Grill It!
Vegetarian

Grill It! Vegetarian

More Than 90 Easy Recipes to Sear, Sizzle, and Savor

Edited by Anne McDowall

COURAGE BOOKS

AN IMPRINT OF RUNNING PRESS
PHILADELPHIA · LONDON

2002 Salamander Ltd
Published by Salamander Books Ltd.
8 Blenheim Court, Brewery Road
London N7 9NY, United Kingdom

© Salamander Books Ltd. 2002

A member of the Chrysalis Group plc

This edition published in the United States in 2002 by Courage Books, an imprint of
Running Press Book Publishers

1 3 5 7 9 8 6 4 2

Library of Congress Cataloguing-in-Publication Number 2001094409

ISBN 0-7624-0996-7

Credits

Commissioning Editor: Stella Caldwell
Project Manager: Anne McDowall
Designer: Mark Holt
Production:Phillip Chamberlain
Color reproduction: Anorax Imaging Ltd
Printed in China

Contents

Introduction

Gone are the days when barbecues were for meat-eaters only. Modern barbecues have evolved to cater for all contemporary tastes and grilling is great for the vegetarian and anyone else wanting a healthy lifestyle. Not only is food at its best and most flavorsome grilled, but this is also a very healthy way to cook, avoiding the need for extra fat and retaining all the goodness and flavor of the food. It's a particularly good way to cook vegetables, whether cooked on the grid, in delicious combinations on skewers, or wrapped in aluminum foil packages and placed directly in the coals.

With a few barbecue basics – a simple grill, some fuel, and basic tools – plus a grasp of simple barbecue cooking techniques, you'll be set to enjoy not only good food, but also the simple pleasure of cooking and eating outdoors. Once you've mastered a few of the many delicious recipes here, you will feel confident to try some ideas of your own. Remember that cooking over coals isn't an exact science – experimentation is part of its appeal.

Grill designs

There are many different types of grills on the market, from simple disposable ones to highly sophisticated gas and electric types and, of course, you can always make your own. If you are new to grilling, or about to buy a new one, it's worth taking a few minutes to consider the different options to decide which would suit you best.

We've mentioned disposable grills, but assuming you want to buy something to use more than once, you may wish to choose a type of portable grill that will be easy to transport. The cheapest and simplest option is a shallow metal bowl on a frame. Such a design has no venting or cover, but it is easy to light and simple to control.

The kettle grill has its own hood, often with adjustable vents, and is suitable for all types of grilling. There are several advantages to choosing a design that has a hood; in bad weather the hood helps protect food while it is cooking and it also prevents spattering and billowing of smoke.

If you want to have lots of barbecues, you might think about building your own – you can use your own materials or buy a ready-to-assemble pack. Either way, the design should have three walls with bars built into the brickwork. Make sure there is enough space for it as a permanent structure in the yard and think carefully about where you site it. It should be far enough away from the house not to be a fire hazard, in a convenient position for people to walk around it, and shielded from strong breezes.

Gas grills contain either vaporizer bars or lava bricks, which heat in the gas flame and absorb juices dripping from the food as it cooks, thus creating flavor. These grills ignite almost instantaneously and require no starter fuel. They retain an even heat and it is possible to have hot coals on one side and moderate on the other if the model has twin switches. Some are very sophisticated wagon models, but all have a small tank of gas, which is cumbersome. However, the advantage with this type of grill is that you can use it at any time of the year.

Electric grills are more popular in some places than in others. As with gas grills, they depend on lava bricks to produce an even heat – they take about 10 minutes to heat – and are usually uncovered. Electric

grills must not be used in the rain, of course, but the more sophisticated models can be used indoors with suitable ducting.

Fuel
Unless you have chosen a gas or electric grill, you will also need to buy suitable fuel. There are two types of coal fuel that can be used: lump charcoal is cheaper, easier to light and burns hotter than its alternative, pressed briquettes. However, once briquettes have been lit, they last a lot longer. Wood can also be used as a fuel, but is more difficult to ignite. If you do want to use wood, choose hardwoods, which burn longer. Allow the flames to die down right before cooking.

Aromatic wood chips are available for use on grills to impart flavors to the food. Oak and hickory wood chips are especially popular, but you may also wish to try more unusual ones, such as mesquite and cherry. You will need to soak wood chips for about

Accessories
The right equipment is a great help for easy grilling and a few tools are worth investing in. Here are some items that you will find useful:

◆ Wooden block or table – useful for keeping implements and food close to hand
◆ Long tools, including tongs and forks – ordinary kitchen tools are not long enough to keep the hands away from the heat source
◆ Wire baskets, such as rectangular, hinged ones (see below right) – to support the food
◆ Skewers – square metal, long wooden or bamboo ones are best

◆ Brushes – for basting food with oil or marinade
◆ Heavy-duty aluminum foil – for wrapping food to cook in the coals or on the grill
◆ Tapers – better than short matches for lighting the grill
◆ Oven gloves – but not the double-handed kind
◆ Apron – a thick one with pockets is ideal
◆ Metal griddle plates – for cooking certain fragile food on
◆ Water sprayer – for dousing the flames if they become too unruly
◆ Stiff wire brush and metal scrapers – for cleaning the grill

30 minutes in cold water, then drain them, before you place them on the ashen coals.

Firelighters, gels or lighting fluid are also invaluable for starting the grill. Make sure you follow the manufacturer's instructions carefully if you are using lighting fluid and never use gasoline, paraffin or other similar flammable liquids to light a grill – apart from affecting the taste of the food they are highly dangerous.

Lighting the grill

Before you light the grill, ensure that it is in the right position (a hot grill is difficult to shift). There is no particular mystique in starting a charcoal fire. Spread a single layer of coals over the grill base, pile up the coals a little and push in firelighters or gel starters. (You don't need to worry about instructions to make a pyramid, as it really isn't necessary.) Light with a taper, rather than matches, and as soon as the fire has caught, spread the coals out a little and add further pieces as necessary.

The coals will probably take 30 to 40 minutes to become hot enough to start cooking over; when the flames have died down and the charcoal is covered with a gray-white ash, it is time to start cooking. (Lava bricks on the other hand only take a few minutes to heat up sufficiently.) Charcoal will burn up for about 1½ hours and occasionally pieces can be added around the edges. Use smaller pieces to poke between the bars of the grid, if necessary.

Checking and adjusting the temperature

Grilling can be done over high, medium or low heat, depending on the type of food. It is easy to adjust the heat on gas and electric grills, but more difficult with the open grid types unless you have a kettle grill with adjustable vents. To test the temperature of the grill, place your open hand over the coals, but be careful when doing so. If you can keep your hand a few inches above the coals for as long as 5 seconds the temperature is low; for 3 to 4 seconds it is medium hot, and for only 2 seconds it is hot.

The right height for cooking is about 2 to 3 inches above the grid. On a lidded grill the heat will be greater when the lid is lowered. If you want to cook over medium heat and the coals have become too hot, either place the food away from the center of the grill and when cooking is completed push it right to the edges to keep warm, or push the coals aside to distribute their heat. To make the fire hotter, poke away the ash, push the coals together and gently blow (you can use a battery operated fan for this – it is invaluable and inexpensive).

Using marinades

Marinating plays a vital part in grilling, as it adds depth of flavor. If food has been marinated in the refrigerator, allow it to come back to room temperature before cooking. Marinades that contain acidic elements, such as vinegar or citrus juice, will tenderize the food. Oils in marinades help prevent food from sticking, while herbs and spices create mouthwatering flavors. Marinating can turn even the simplest vegetable into something special.

Cooking in foil

Wrapping food in heavy-duty or double-thickness aluminum foil prevents the outside of the food from burning before the inside is cooked and keeps the juices trapped inside. For foods that require some browning, leave some space between the covering and the food, otherwise wrap into tight packages. Make sure the edges of the foil are firmly sealed.

Cooking in the coals

This is also known as cooking in the embers, and the food can be either wrapped in heavy-duty aluminum foil and dropped into the coals, or, in the case of some foods, even placed directly in the coals without any wrapping.

Using skewers

Most skewered food is marinated first. During cooking the food should be brushed either with oil, or with a marinade or baste, and the skewers will need to be turned frequently during cooking. Wooden handles on skewers don't get as hot as metal ones. Look for long skewers, which go fully across the grill and hold enough for two to three servings. Make sure wooden handles protrude from the edge of the grill pan to prevent scorching. Bamboo skewers are good for smaller portions, but need soaking for an hour before you use them, or they will burn. It is generally best to oil metal skewers before use. Serve food on the skewers or transfer onto the plates with a fork.

Grilling

All barbecues can be used for grilling on top of the flame – indeed this is the cooking method generally associated with barbecues. Most of the recipes in this book could also be cooked in a conventional broiler if the weather drives you indoors, although the true barbecue flavor will be lacking.

Skillet or pan cooking

A heavy-bottomed skillet, griddle or pan can be used over a grill in the same way as on the top of a conventional stove. Merely grease the surface of the skillet and cooking becomes a cross between baking over the grill and shallow frying. Should the food start cooking too quickly, just move the skillet to the side of the grill. Coals need to be very hot for successful cooking in this way.

Cooking times

Although times are given in the recipes, they must be regarded as a guide only. There are so many variables – cooking times will be affected by the thickness of the food, the type and heat of the coals, the position of the grid, the weather, and so on. One of the great pleasures of barbecuing is that it is a chance to experiment.

Cleaning up

When you have finally finished with the grill, push the coals away from the center and they will die down. Cleaning the grill is best done while it is still hot. Use a metal scraper or stiff wire brush to dislodge food residues into the fire. If bits of food remain, remove the grid when it is cold and wash it in hot soapy water. When the embers are completely cold, sift away surplus ash and cover the grill with the lid for use next time.

Safety checklist

- Always place the grill on an even surface and away from trees, buildings or fences.
- Never use gasoline or similar flammable liquid to light the grill, and keep boxes of matches away from the flames.
- Have a bottle of water handy to douse the flames if necessary.
- Once the grill is fired, do not leave it unattended and keep children away from it.
- Always use long-handled tongs when handling food on the grill.
- Keep food to be grilled in the refrigerator until you are ready to cook it, then keep it covered and out of the sun.
- Allow embers to cool completely (for several hours) before disposing of them.
- Allow trolley grills to cool completely before packing them away.

Appetizers and Snacks

Radicchio with Mozzarella

MAKES 4 SERVINGS

6 ANCHOVIES IN OLIVE OIL

*2 GARLIC CLOVES,
CUT INTO SLIVERS*

*2 LARGE HEADS RADICCHIO,
CUT IN HALF LENGTHWISE*

SALT AND FRESHLY GROUND BLACK PEPPER

*1 CUP (4 OUNCES) SHREDDED
MOZZARELLA CHEESE*

LEMON SLICES, TO GARNISH

◆ Drain anchovies, reserving oil, and chop. Push garlic slivers and anchovy pieces between radicchio leaves.

◆ Grill radicchio halves, cut side up, over medium coals 5 minutes, or until the underside of the radicchio softens and begins to brown. Remove from the grill. Season with salt and pepper.

◆ Place each radicchio half, cut side up, on a piece of heavy-duty aluminum foil, drizzle with a little oil reserved from anchovies, and arrange shredded mozzarella on top.

◆ Seal packages and replace on grill 10 minutes, or until mozzarella is melting.

◆ Garnish with lemon slices and serve immediately.

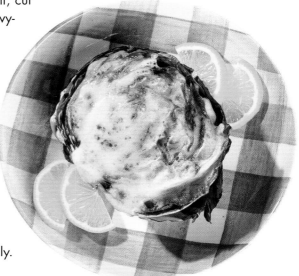

Chive and Garlic Bread

MAKES 6 SERVINGS

1 FRENCH BAGUETTE

3 GARLIC CLOVES

¼ TEASPOON SALT

1 STICK (4 OUNCES) BUTTER

*2 TABLESPOONS CHOPPED
FRESH CHIVES*

◆ Slice baguette diagonally and deeply at about ¾-inch intervals, but do not cut through completely.

◆ Peel garlic, place on a piece of waxed paper, sprinkle with salt, and crush with flat side of a table knife. Soften butter, blend in garlic and mix in chives. Spread garlic butter between slices of bread, covering both sides generously.

◆ Reshape the loaf and wrap securely in heavy-duty aluminum foil. Grill over hot coals 10 to 15 minutes, turning package over several times. Open foil and serve at once.

Polenta with Vegetables

MAKES 4 SERVINGS

DASH SALT

¾ CUP (4 OUNCES) POLENTA

1 TABLESPOON (½ OUNCE) BUTTER

DASH FRESHLY GROUND BLACK PEPPER

1 SMALL EGGPLANT, THINLY SLICED

1 ZUCCHINI, THINLY SLICED

½ CUP OLIVE OIL

*1 RED BELL PEPPER,
QUARTERED AND SEEDED*

BASIL LEAVES, TO GARNISH

◆ Place 1¼ pints water in a pan and bring to a boil. Add a dash of salt then pour in polenta in a fine, steady stream, stirring vigorously with a wooden spoon. Simmer gently 5 to 10 minutes, stirring frequently, until polenta is thick and no longer grainy. Remove the pan from heat and stir in butter and black pepper.

◆ Turn polenta onto an oiled baking sheet or wooden board and spread out to a thickness of ¼ to ½ inch. Cool, cover and refrigerate 1 hour. With a 2½- to 3-inch pastry cutter, cut polenta into 8 circles.

◆ Brush eggplant and zucchini with oil and grill until browned on both sides. Keep warm. Grill bell pepper quarters and peel away and dispose of blackened skins. Keep warm.

◆ Brush polenta circles with oil and grill 3 to 4 minutes on each side until lightly browned and crisp.

◆ Place a polenta circle on each of 4 serving plates and arrange vegetable slices on top. Season with salt and pepper and top with another polenta circle. Garnish with basil to serve.

Tomato and Olive Oil Bruschetta

MAKES 6 SERVINGS

6 LARGE RIPE TOMATOES, THINLY SLICED

6 LARGE BASIL LEAVES, SHREDDED

⅓ CUP EXTRA VIRGIN OLIVE OIL

SALT AND FRESHLY GROUND BLACK PEPPER

1 SMALL CIABATTA LOAF
(ITALIAN OLIVE OIL BREAD)
OR FRENCH BAGUETTE

2 GARLIC CLOVES, HALVED

◆ Place tomatoes, basil, olive oil and seasonings in a dish, stir to combine, and let marinate 30 minutes.

◆ Slice bread in half lengthwise and grill on both sides 1 to 2 minutes until lightly golden.

◆ Rub garlic all over toast and top with marinated tomato mixture. Cut into fingers and serve.

Tofu with Miso Sauce

MAKES 4 SERVINGS

1 POUND 2 OUNCES FIRM TOFU

TOASTED SESAME SEEDS,
TO SPRINKLE

BAMBOO LEAVES,
TO GARNISH (OPTIONAL)

MISO SAUCE

3½ OUNCES MISO

1 EGG YOLK

1 TABLESPOON SAKE

1 TABLESPOON MIRIN

1 TABLESPOON SUGAR

¼ CUP DASHI (SEE NOTE)

JUICE ¼ LIME

◆ Wrap each tofu cake in a clean dish cloth and place a light weight, such as a plate, on top to squeeze out water. Let stand at least 1 hour.

◆ To make miso sauce, place miso in a bowl and blend in egg yolk, sake, mirin and sugar. Place bowl over a pan of simmering water.

◆ Gradually add dashi to pan and stir until sauce becomes thick but not too hard, then stir in lime juice.

◆ Remove from heat immediately and cool to room temperature (it will keep well in the refrigerator, if wished).

◆ Unwrap tofu cakes and cut into 2 x ¾ x ½-inch slices. Skewer each of the slices lengthwise with 2 bamboo skewers. Place on a grill over hot coals a few minutes until lightly browned on one side only.

◆ Remove from heat and, using a butter knife, thickly spread toasted side with miso sauce. Sprinkle with toasted sesame seeds.

◆ Replace skewers on grill 1 to 2 minutes. Serve hot on skewers on a bed of bamboo leaves as a garnish, if desired.

Note: For instant dashi, mix dashi-no-moto (freeze-dried dashi powder) with water following the package directions.

North African Stuffed Vine Leaves

MAKES 4 SERVINGS

*1 TABLESPOON CHOPPED
FRESH MINT*

¼ TEASPOON GROUND CORIANDER

DASH GROUND CUMIN

SALT AND FRESHLY GROUND BLACK PEPPER

*4 GREEN ONIONS,
FINELY CHOPPED*

*1 SMALL NECTARINE OR PEACH,
PITTED AND FINELY CHOPPED*

8 LARGE VINE LEAVES

OLIVE OIL, FOR BRUSHING

*4 OUNCES GOAT'S CHEESE
OR LOW-FAT CREAM CHEESE*

*CRISP GREEN SALAD, TO SERVE
(OPTIONAL)*

◆ In a small bowl, mix together mint, ground coriander, ground cumin and salt and pepper. Add green onions and nectarine or peach and stir well to coat evenly in spice mixture.

◆ Wash and dry vine leaves, arrange in pairs on serving plates and brush top leaves with olive oil.

◆ Cut cheese into 4 equal slices. Place a slice of cheese at one end of each pair of leaves and top with nectarine mixture.

◆ Carefully fold leaves over cheese until completely covered and secure with cocktail sticks.

◆ Brush parcels with oil, and grill over hot coals 4 to 5 minutes.

◆ Transfer to serving plates, carefully remove cocktail sticks and serve at once with a crisp green salad.

Grilled Goat's Cheese

2 TABLESPOONS OLIVE OIL

2 TABLESPOONS WALNUT OR HAZELNUT OIL

*1 TEASPOON BLACK PEPPERCORNS,
COARSELY CRUSHED*

*1 TABLESPOON CHOPPED
FRESH THYME*

*4 GOAT'S CHEESES OR 4 SLICES
GOAT'S CHEESE*

8 OUNCES FRISÉE LETTUCE

½ CUP (1 OUNCE) ARUGULA

4 THIN SLICES FRENCH BREAD

1 TABLESPOON RED WINE VINEGAR

½ TEASPOON DIJON-STYLE MUSTARD

◆ Mix together olive and walnut (or hazelnut) oils, peppercorns and thyme. Place cheese in a small shallow dish, pour over oil mixture and turn cheese in oil to coat.

◆ Marinate in refrigerator 12 to 14 hours, or overnight, turning cheese occasionally.

◆ Arrange frisée and arugula leaves on serving plates. Remove cheese from oil to a plate, reserving oil.

◆ Brush both sides of each slice of bread with a little reserved oil. Toast one side of bread slices over a hot grill.

◆ Remove from the grill and top toasted side with cheese. Replace on the grill over hot coals until cheese is beginning to melt.

◆ Whisk together vinegar and mustard then slowly whisk in reserved oil. Pour over salad leaves, top with grilled goat's cheese and serve immediately.

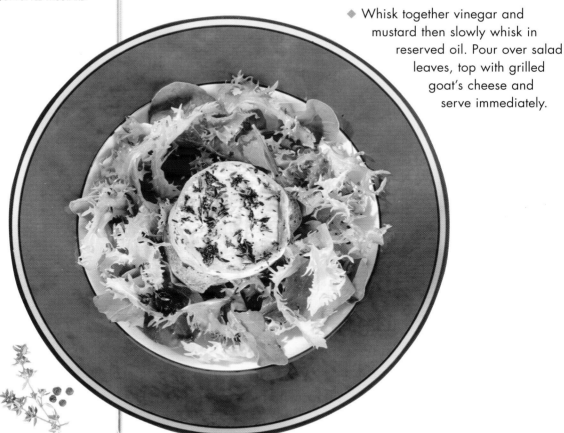

Goat's Cheese, Leek and Walnut Bruschetta

MAKES 6 SERVINGS

6 SLICES FRENCH BREAD,
SLICED DIAGONALLY

3 TABLESPOONS OLIVE OIL

SIX 1½-OUNCE SLICES SOFT
GOAT'S CHEESE

FRESHLY GROUND BLACK PEPPER

LEEK AND WALNUT TOPPING

2 TABLESPOONS OLIVE OIL

1 SMALL OR ½ MEDIUM LEEK,
THINLY SLICED

2 TABLESPOONS (½ OUNCE) WALNUTS,
COARSELY CHOPPED

◆ To make topping, heat oil in a pan and cook and stir leeks 3 minutes, or until soft.

◆ Remove from heat, stir in chopped walnuts and season with salt and pepper to taste. Set aside until required.

◆ Brush both sides of bread slices with 2 tablespoons of olive oil. Place bread on grill over hot coals and toast 2 minutes on one side only.

◆ Remove from the grill and divide leek and walnut topping between toasted sides of bread slices. Top each with a slice of goat's cheese and drizzle with remaining olive oil. Grind over some black pepper.

◆ Return bruschetta to grill and cook 3 to 4 more minutes until cheese begins to melt. Serve at once.

Crispy Potato Skins

SERVES 5 TO 8

4 LARGE BAKING POTATOES

1 STICK (4 OUNCES) BUTTER

SALT AND FRESHLY GROUND BLACK PEPPER

◆ Scrub potatoes and pat dry with paper towels. Prick skin in several places, wrap tightly in heavy-duty aluminum foil and cook directly in hot coals 45 minutes to 1 hour.

◆ Halve potatoes lengthwise and scoop out flesh. (Reserve to use for mashing, or for potato salad if firm enough.) Cut potato skins into 1-inch wide strips.

◆ Melt butter and season to taste with salt and pepper. Dip potato skins into melted butter, then thread onto skewers and grill over hot coals 5 to 7 minutes.

◆ Serve hot.

Peanut Tomatoes

8 SLICES WHITE BREAD

4 LARGE TOMATOES

*SALT AND FRESHLY GROUND
BLACK PEPPER*

FEW DROPS WORCESTERSHIRE SAUCE

*2 TEASPOONS CHOPPED
FRESH BASIL*

*2 TEASPOONS CHOPPED
FRESH PARSLEY*

*1 TABLESPOON GRATED
PARMESAN CHEESE*

*⅓ CUP (2 OUNCES) ROASTED UNSALTED
PEANUTS, FINELY GROUND*

1 TABLESPOON BUTTER

*BASIL OR PARSLEY LEAVES,
TO GARNISH*

◆ To make fried croûton 'bracelets', cut 8 rounds from slices of bread and use a slightly smaller cutter to remove centers. Shallow fry in oil. Drain thoroughly and set aside. (These can be made ahead of time, frozen, and re-crisped on the grill at the last minute.)

◆ Rinse and dry tomatoes and halve crosswise. Season cut surfaces of tomatoes with salt and pepper. Sprinkle with a few drops of Worcestershire sauce.

◆ Top tomatoes with basil and parsley mixed together, then sprinkle with grated Parmesan cheese. Cover with ground peanuts and add a small piece of butter to each one.

◆ Loosely wrap tomato halves separately in aluminum foil. Place cut sides up on the grid and grill over hot coals 20 to 25 minutes until tomatoes are soft.

◆ Remove from foil wrappings and place each tomato in center of a fried croûton bracelet. Garnish with basil or parsley leaves.

Eggplant and Cheese Packages

1 LARGE EGGPLANT

½ CUP EXTRA VIRGIN OLIVE OIL

SALT AND FRESHLY GROUND BLACK PEPPER

*2 CIABATTA LOAVES
(ITALIAN OLIVE OIL BREAD)
OR 2 FRENCH BAGUETTES*

*2 TABLESPOONS CHOPPED
FRESH BASIL*

2 RIPE PLUM TOMATOES

4 OUNCES MOZZARELLA CHEESE

◆ Remove and discard stalk from eggplant and slice lengthwise into four long slices, discarding 2 outer edges (you should be left with 4 flat pieces).

◆ Brush each piece on both sides with half the olive oil and season well with salt and pepper.

◆ Cook eggplant slices on the grill a few minutes on each side until pale golden and soft.

◆ Slice each loaf lengthwise in 2, then into 4 chunks. Mix together basil and remaining olive oil and use to brush cut sides of bread.

◆ Slice each tomato into 4 and cut mozzarella into 4 thick slices. Layer tomato and mozzarella to produce 4 stacks, each consisting of one piece of cheese sandwiched between 2 slices of tomato.

◆ Wrap a slice of eggplant around each cheese and tomato stack and place each parcel between 2 slices of ciabatta bread.

◆ Wrap each package in a piece of heavy-duty aluminum foil, turning over edges to seal in filling.

◆ Place packages on the grill over hot coals 4 to 5 minutes on each side, or until bread is warmed through and cheese has begun to melt. Serve at once.

Fennel with Feta and Pears

MAKES 4 SERVINGS

2 FENNEL BULBS

¼ CUP OLIVE OIL

6 OUNCES FETA CHEESE

1 RIPE PEAR

4 SUN-DRIED TOMATOES IN OIL,
DRAINED AND SLICED

8 PITTED RIPE OLIVES

1 TABLESPOON SHREDDED
BASIL LEAVES

1 TEASPOON LEMON JUICE

½ TEASPOON CLEAR HONEY

SALT AND FRESHLY GROUND BLACK PEPPER

◆ Trim fennel, discarding any damaged outer leaves. Cut each bulb lengthwise into 6 thin slices.

◆ Brush fennel slices with a little of olive oil and grill 2 to 3 minutes on each side until browned and just tender. Leave to cool slightly.

◆ Slice feta and quarter, core and thinly slice pear. Arrange fennel, cheese and pear slices on serving plates and top with tomatoes, olives and basil.

◆ Blend remaining oil, lemon juice, honey and seasonings together, drizzle over salad and serve.

Vine Leaves with Feta, Olives and Tomatoes

MAKES 4 SERVINGS

8 LARGE VINE LEAVES

2 TABLESPOONS OLIVE OIL

4 OUNCES FETA CHEESE,
CUT INTO SMALL CUBES

16 SMALL RIPE OLIVES

8 CHERRY TOMATOES, HALVED

8 SPRIGS FRESH OREGANO

FRESHLY GROUND BLACK PEPPER

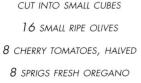

◆ Rinse vine leaves and dry them on paper towels. Lay them flat on a surface and brush each leaf with a little olive oil.

◆ Divide feta, olives, tomatoes and oregano evenly among leaves, placing them in the center of each leaf. Grind over some black pepper and fold leaves around filling to enclose it completely. Secure vine-leaf packages with cocktail sticks.

◆ Brush outside of packages with remaining oil and cook them on a prepared grill 4 to 5 minutes, or until cheese has begun to melt. (They do not need to be turned, but do keep skewered side of packages upright, away from coals.)

◆ Serve 2 vine-leaf packages to each person. Peel away vine leaves and eat filling. (The leaves are purely to enclose filling and are not intended to be eaten.)

Stuffed Chile Peppers

12 LARGE FRESH RED OR GREEN CHILES

4 SUN-DRIED TOMATOES IN OIL, DRAINED AND FINELY CHOPPED

½ CUP (5 OUNCES) MILD SOFT GOAT'S CHEESE

2 GREEN ONIONS, WHITE PART ONLY, FINELY CHOPPED

2 TEASPOONS FINELY CHOPPED FRESH MINT

1 TEASPOON FINELY CHOPPED FRESH BASIL

SALT AND FRESHLY GROUND BLACK PEPPER

3 TABLESPOONS EXTRA VIRGIN OLIVE OIL

1 TABLESPOON WHITE WINE VINEGAR

FRESH MINT LEAVES, TO GARNISH

◆ Grill chiles over hot coals 5 to 8 minutes, turning occasionally, until skins are evenly blistered and charred. Transfer to a plastic bag for a few minutes, then peel away and discard skins.

◆ Make a slit along length of each chile. Carefully rinse off seeds under cold running water. Pat chiles dry with paper towels.

◆ To make filling, in a small bowl, mix together sun-dried tomatoes, goat's cheese, green onions, mint, basil, salt and pepper.

◆ Divide filling between chiles and arrange on a serving plate. Drizzle over olive oil and vinegar.

◆ Chill in refrigerator at least 30 minutes. Serve garnished with mint leaves.

Moroccan Spiced Garlic Bread

MAKES 6 SERVINGS

2 SMALL FRENCH BAGUETTES

1½ STICKS (6 OUNCES) BUTTER, SOFTENED

2 GARLIC CLOVES, CRUSHED

1 TABLESPOON TOMATO PASTE

1 TABLESPOON CHOPPED CILANTRO

1 TABLESPOON CHOPPED FRESH PARSLEY

½ TEASPOON GROUND CUMIN

½ TEASPOON GROUND PAPRIKA

DASH CAYENNE PEPPER

SALT, TO TASTE

◆ Cut baguettes into ½-inch slices, without cutting right through.

◆ Cream together butter, garlic, tomato paste, cilantro, parsley, cumin, paprika, cayenne pepper and salt. Spread a little of this spiced butter between each bread slice. Spread any remaining butter all over bread.

◆ Wrap baguettes in heavy-duty aluminum foil and turn edges over to seal.

◆ Place foil packages at the edges of the grill and cook over hot coals 5 minutes. Turn packages over and cook 5 more minutes.

◆ Serve piping hot.

Feta Cheese Kabobs

7 OUNCES FETA CHEESE

¼ RED BELL PEPPER

¼ YELLOW BELL PEPPER

1 ZUCCHINI

¼ EGGPLANT

THYME SPRIGS, TO GARNISH

MARINADE

1½ TABLESPOONS OLIVE OIL

1 TABLESPOON RASPBERRY VINEGAR

1 TEASPOON PINK PEPPERCORNS, CRUSHED

1 TEASPOON CLEAR HONEY

½ TEASPOON DIJON-STYLE MUSTARD

2 TEASPOONS CHOPPED FRESH THYME

¼ TEASPOON SALT

½ TEASPOON FRESHLY GROUND BLACK PEPPER

◆ To make marinade, place olive oil, vinegar, pink peppercorns, honey, mustard, thyme, salt and pepper in a large bowl. Stir mixture together with a wooden spoon until thoroughly blended.

◆ Cut feta cheese, peppers, zucchini, and eggplant into bite-size pieces. Add to marinade, stir well to coat evenly, cover with plastic wrap and refrigerate at least 1 hour.

◆ Thread one piece of each ingredient onto wooden cocktail sticks. Just before serving, cook on the grill 2 to 3 minutes, until vegetables are just tender.

◆ Arrange kabobs on a serving plate, garnished with sprigs of thyme.

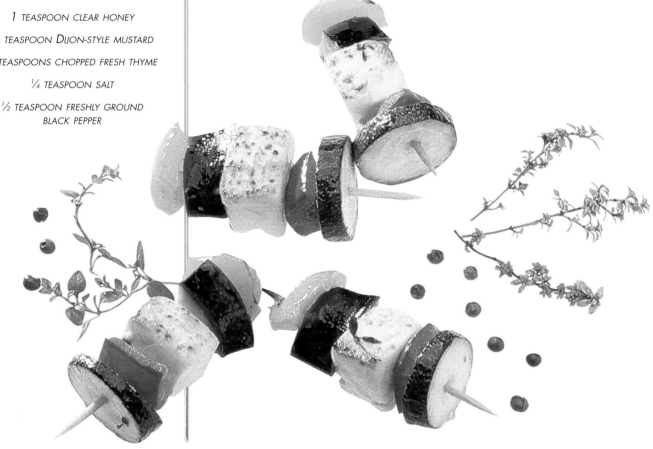

Eggplant, Mushroom and Hazelnut Salad

MAKES 4 SERVINGS

1 SMALL EGGPLANT

3 TABLESPOONS OLIVE OIL

*16 SHIITAKE MUSHROOMS
(ABOUT 4 OUNCES)*

*8 CUPS (ABOUT 1 POUND)
MIXED SALAD LEAVES*

*1½ TABLESPOONS CHOPPED
CILANTRO*

*¼ CUP (1 OUNCE) HAZELNUTS,
TOASTED AND COARSELY CHOPPED*

DRESSING

⅓ CUP OLIVE OIL

1 TEASPOON SESAME OIL

2 TEASPOONS LIGHT SOY SAUCE

1 TABLESPOON BALSAMIC VINEGAR

½ TEASPOON SUGAR

FRESHLY GROUND BLACK PEPPER

◆ Cut eggplant into thin slices, brush with oil and cook on the grill 2 to 3 minutes on each side, until charred and softened. Let cool.

◆ Thinly slice mushrooms. Heat remaining oil in a small skillet and stir-fry mushrooms over medium heat 3 to 4 minutes until tender. Drain on paper towels and let cool.

◆ Wash salad leaves, shake off excess water and place in a large bowl. Sprinkle over cilantro and nuts.

◆ To make dressing, blend together olive and sesame oils, soy sauce, balsamic vinegar, sugar and black pepper, until well mixed.

◆ Add eggplant and mushrooms to salad, pour over dressing, toss well and serve at once.

Vegetables

Chargrilled Artichokes

⅓ CUP OLIVE OIL

1 GARLIC CLOVE, CRUSHED

*2 TABLESPOONS CHOPPED
FRESH PARSLEY*

SALT AND FRESHLY GROUND BLACK PEPPER

6 BABY ARTICHOKES

FLAT-LEAF PARSLEY, TO GARNISH

RED BELL PEPPER SAUCE

1 TABLESPOON OLIVE OIL

1 SMALL ONION, CHOPPED

2 RED BELL PEPPERS, DICED

1 CUP VEGETABLE STOCK

◆ In a small bowl, mix together olive oil, garlic, parsley and salt and pepper. Set aside.

◆ To make red pepper sauce, heat oil in a saucepan, add onion and cook 5 minutes until soft.

◆ Add red peppers and cook over a low heat for 5 minutes, then pour in stock, bring to a boil and simmer 10 minutes.

◆ Push peppers through a sieve or purée in a food processor or blender. Season with salt and freshly ground black pepper to taste.

◆ Trim bottoms of artichokes and remove any tough outer leaves. Cut artichokes in half lengthwise and immediately brush with seasoned oil.

◆ Lay artichoke halves on the grill over medium coals and grill about 10 minutes, turning once, or until browned on both sides.

◆ Reheat sauce. Drizzle artichokes with remaining seasoned oil, garnish with parsley and serve with red pepper sauce.

Greek Grilled Vegetables

MAKES 4 SERVINGS

2 BABY EGGPLANTS

4 BABY ZUCCHINI

1 RED BELL PEPPER

1 YELLOW BELL PEPPER

1 FENNEL BULB

4 OUNCES FETA CHEESE

1 TABLESPOON LEMON JUICE

SALT AND FRESHLY GROUND BLACK PEPPER

*ZUCCHINI FLOWERS,
TO GARNISH*

MARINADE:

⅔ CUP OLIVE OIL

2 GARLIC CLOVES, CRUSHED

1 TEASPOON CHOPPED FRESH PARSLEY

1 TEASPOON CHOPPED FRESH MINT

*1 TEASPOON CHOPPED
FRESH OREGANO*

◆ To make marinade, mix together olive oil, garlic, parsley, mint and oregano in a small bowl.

◆ Cut eggplants and zucchini lengthwise in half. Cut peppers into quarters and remove seeds. Quarter and slice fennel.

◆ Cut feta into small cubes and place in a bowl. Add a little of the marinade and mix gently.

◆ Place eggplants, zucchini, pepper and fennel in another bowl with remaining marinade, mix together and let stand 1 hour.

◆ Grill vegetables, turning and brushing with marinade every few minutes, 10 minutes, or until tender and flecked brown. Let cool.

◆ Arrange vegetables on a serving plate. Drizzle with lemon juice and season with salt and pepper. Scatter over feta, garnish with zucchini flowers and serve.

Vegetables with Skordalia

2 YELLOW OR RED BELL PEPPERS,
SEEDED AND QUARTERED

1 OR 2 BEETS,
SCRUBBED AND THINLY SLICED

1 OR 2 JERUSALEM ARTICHOKES, SCRUBBED
AND THINLY SLICED

1 EGGPLANT, THINLY SLICED

2 SMALL ZUCCHINI,
SLICED LENGTHWISE

1 SMALL HEAD RADICCHIO,
CUT INTO THIN WEDGES

1 FENNEL BULB,
THINLY SLICED LENGTHWISE

8 TO 10 SPEARS (8 OUNCES)
ASPARAGUS SPEARS, TRIMMED

¼ CUP LEMON CITRUS OIL
(SEE NOTE) OR OLIVE OIL

1 CUP SKORDALIA
(SEE PAGE 90)

◆ Brush all vegetables with citrus or olive oil and grill over hot coals until charred and tender. The cooking times will vary depending on the vegetable.

◆ Arrange vegetables on a large platter and drizzle over any remaining oil. Serve at room temperature with skordalia.

Note: Citrus oil is easy to make but is best made in advance to allow flavors to infuse. Place 4 strips of lemon peel into a clean jar and pour over 1¼ cups olive oil. It will keep up to two weeks if stored in the refrigerator.

Chargrilled Bell Peppers

*6 LARGE BELL PEPPERS,
RED, YELLOW AND ORANGE*

DRESSING

*¼ CUP HAZELNUT
OR OLIVE OIL*

2 TEASPOONS BALSAMIC VINEGAR

*1 LARGE GARLIC CLOVE,
CHOPPED*

SALT AND FRESHLY GROUND BLACK PEPPER

*2 TABLESPOONS CHOPPED
FRESH BASIL*

◆ Place peppers on the grid over hot coals and grill, turning frequently until skins blister and become charred.

◆ Place peppers in a plastic bag and let cool and soften 30 minutes.

◆ Peel peppers and discard skins and seeds, over a bowl to reserve juices. Cut flesh into thick slices.

◆ Pour pepper juices into a bowl and blend in hazelnut or olive oil, balsamic vinegar, garlic, salt and freshly ground black pepper.

◆ Pour dressing over peppers and sprinkle over basil. Serve peppers warm or cold.

Capered New Potatoes

MAKES 4 TO 6 SERVINGS

8 (1 POUND) NEW POTATOES

3 TABLESPOONS CAPERS

*¾ STICK (3 OUNCES) BUTTER,
SOFTENED*

PARSLEY LEAVES, TO GARNISH

◆ Scrub potatoes well, then boil in their skins in salted water 10 minutes. Drain and let cool slightly.

◆ Finely chop capers and blend with butter. Make a deep slit in each potato and fill with caper butter.

◆ Tightly wrap each potato in individual squares of heavy-duty aluminum foil and grill over hot coals 10 to 15 minutes.

◆ Garnish with leaves of parsley to serve.

Baked Sweet Potatoes with Garlic and Thyme

MAKES 4 SERVINGS

3 (1½ POUNDS) SWEET POTATOES,
PEELED AND CUT INTO SMALL CHUNKS

12 UNPEELED GARLIC CLOVES

12 SPRIGS THYME

¾ STICK (3 OUNCES) BUTTER,
FINELY CHOPPED

SALT AND FRESHLY GROUND BLACK PEPPER

◆ Cut 6 large squares of double-thickness aluminum foil. Divide potatoes among foil squares. To each pile of potatoes add 2 garlic cloves, 2 sprigs thyme, a few pieces of butter and plenty salt and freshly ground black pepper.

◆ Pull the edges of the foil up and over potatoes to completely seal the fillings in packages.

◆ Place packages on the grill over hot coals and cook 20 to 25 minutes, until potatoes are tender. Serve straight from the foil.

Foil-baked Mushrooms

MAKES 6 SERVINGS

18 SMALL FLAT-CAP MUSHROOMS

¾ STICK (3 OUNCES) BUTTER, SOFTENED

1 GARLIC CLOVE, CRUSHED

1 TABLESPOON CHOPPED
FRESH SAGE

GRATED PEEL 1 LEMON

SALT AND FRESHLY GROUND BLACK PEPPER

◆ Cut 6 large squares of double-thickness aluminum foil. Place 3 mushrooms in the center of each double layer of foil.

◆ Cream together butter, garlic, sage, lemon peel and salt and pepper and spread about a heaped teaspoonful over each mushroom.

◆ Pull the edges of the foil up over the mushrooms and turn over to seal fillings.

◆ Place the foil packages on the grid over hot coals 6 to 8 minutes until mushrooms are tender and juicy. Serve straight from the foil.

Yams and Plantains with Hot Pepper Mayonnaise

FOUR 5-OUNCE SLICES YAM,
PEELED

FOUR 3-OUNCE THICK SLICES
HALF-RIPE PLANTAIN,
WITH SKINS LEFT INTACT

CORN OIL, FOR BRUSHING

SALT AND FRESHLY GROUND BLACK PEPPER

HOT PEPPER MAYONNAISE

⅓ CUP MAYONNAISE

2 TABLESPOONS CHOPPED
FRESH THYME

1 TEASPOON SEEDED AND
FINELY CHOPPED HOT JAMAICAN CHILE

1 TABLESPOON FRESHLY SQUEEZED
LIME JUICE

SALT AND FRESHLY GROUND BLACK PEPPER

◆ Cook yam slices in boiling salted water 15 minutes or until tender. Drain and set aside until required.

◆ To make hot pepper mayonnaise, mix together in a bowl mayonnaise, thyme, chile, lime juice, salt and pepper. Refrigerate until required.

◆ Brush yam and plantain slices all over with corn oil and season with salt and freshly ground black pepper.

◆ Cook vegetable slices on the grill over hot coals, turning them occasionally until they are tender and charred on the outside. The plantains will be ready to serve in about 12 minutes and the yams in about 15.

◆ Serve at once with hot pepper mayonnaise.

Vegetables with Tahini Dressing

2 SWEET POTATOES,
PEELED AND CUT INTO 4 SLICES

1 CELERIAC,
PEELED AND CUT INTO 4 SLICES

12 OUNCES PUMPKIN,
PEELED AND CUT INTO 4 WEDGES

2 MEDIUM PARSNIPS,
PEELED AND HALVED LENGTHWISE

⅓ CUP OLIVE OIL
FOR BRUSHING

SALT AND FRESHLY GROUND BLACK PEPPER

TAHINI DRESSING

3 TABLESPOONS LIGHT TAHINI

3 TABLESPOONS MAYONNAISE

2 TABLESPOONS OLIVE OIL

¼ TEASPOON PAPRIKA

2 GARLIC CLOVES,
CRUSHED

2 GREEN ONIONS,
CHOPPED

2 TEASPOONS LEMON JUICE

SALT AND FRESHLY GROUND
BLACK PEPPER

◆ To make tahini dressing, mix together in a bowl light tahini, mayonnaise, olive oil, paprika, garlic, green onions, lemon juice, salt and pepper. Refrigerate until required.

◆ Cook different types of root vegetables individually in boiling water until they are just tender. Celeriac will take about 12 minutes to cook, sweet potato 10 minutes, parsnip 8 minutes and pumpkin 6 minutes. Drain cooked vegetables and dry them on paper towels.

◆ Brush vegetables all over with olive oil and season generously with salt and freshly ground black pepper.

◆ Cook vegetables on the oiled grid of the grill over hot coals about 6 minutes on each side, turning them halfway through cooking and brushing occasionally with oil.

◆ Serve with tahini dressing.

Sesame Zucchini

MAKES 6 SERVINGS

6 LARGE ZUCCHINI

SESAME OIL, TO BRUSH

DRESSING

⅓ CUP SESAME OIL

2 TABLESPOONS LEMON JUICE

1 TABLESPOON CHOPPED
FRESH ROSEMARY

DASH SUGAR

SALT AND FRESHLY GROUND BLACK PEPPER

◆ To make dressing, blend together sesame oil, lemon juice, rosemary, sugar, salt and pepper.

◆ Cut each zucchini into 4 thick slices and brush with sesame oil.

◆ Cook zucchini on the grid over hot coals 2 to 3 minutes on each side until browned.

◆ Place in a shallow serving dish and pour dressing over it. Serve zucchini hot or cold.

Whole Tomatoes in Wine

MAKES 8 SERVINGS

8 FIRM TOMATOES

8 TEASPOONS RED WINE

SALT AND FRESHLY GROUND BLACK PEPPER

WATERCRESS OR LETTUCE LEAVES,
TO SERVE

◆ Cut 8 large squares of heavy-duty aluminum foil. Cup each tomato in foil but do not completely enclose.

◆ Pour 1 teaspoon wine over each tomato and season each to taste with salt and pepper. Mold foil around tomatoes to prevent juices escaping.

◆ Place foil packages on the side of the grill over medium coals and cook about 10-15 minutes. Unwrap and transfer to serving plates, spooning wine-flavored juices over tomatoes.

◆ Serve on a bed of watercress or lettuce leaves.

Japanese Grilled Eggplant

*4 EGGPLANTS,
STEMS REMOVED*

*VEGETABLE OIL,
FOR FRYING*

*1½ TO 2-INCH PIECE FRESH GINGER,
PEELED AND GRATED*

*8 FRESH MINT LEAVES,
FINELY SHREDDED*

GINGER SAUCE

⅓ CUP DASHI (SEE NOTE)

2 TABLESPOONS SHOYU

*2 TABLESPOONS MIRIN
OR 2 TEASPOONS SUGAR*

2 TABLESPOONS SAKE

SESAME SAUCE

3 TABLESPOONS WHITE SESAME SEEDS

*3 TABLESPOONS DASHI
(SEE NOTE)*

1½ TABLESPOONS SHOYU

½ TABLESPOON SUGAR

DASH SALT

Note: For instant dashi, mix dashi-no-moto (freeze-dried dashi powder) with water following the package instructions.

◆ To make ginger sauce, place dashi, shoyu, mirin or sugar and sake in a pan and boil 1 minute. Remove from heat and set aside.

◆ To make sesame sauce, toast sesame seeds in a small dry saucepan, then grind them into a paste in a mortar. Mix in dashi and shoyu and season with sugar and a dash of salt.

◆ Slice eggplants lengthwise into quarters and cook on the grill over hot coals a few minutes on each side until softened.

◆ Place 2 eggplant slices on each of 8 small plates. Arrange grated ginger and mint slices on top of 4 of the plates and add ginger sauce. Pour sesame sauce over eggplant slices on the other 4 plates. Serve one of each type to each person.

Spiced Corn

4 EARS CORN, HUSKS REMOVED

2 TABLESPOONS OLIVE OIL

1/2 TEASPOON CAYENNE PEPPER

SALT AND FRESHLY GROUND BLACK PEPPER

CHILI BUTTER

3/4 STICK (3 OUNCES) BUTTER, SOFTENED

2 TABLESPOONS COARSELY CHOPPED FRESH CILANTRO

2 TEASPOONS FINELY CHOPPED FRESH RED CHILE

SALT AND FRESHLY GROUND BLACK PEPPER

◆ To prepare chili butter, mix together softened butter, cilantro, chile, salt and pepper in a small bowl until thoroughly combined.

◆ Roll butter into a sausage shape on a piece of plastic wrap or waxed paper. Roll up to form a cylinder and refrigerate to harden butter.

◆ Cook corn in plenty of boiling, salted water about 15 minutes until it is tender, then drain.

◆ In a bowl mix together olive oil, cayenne and seasoning. Brush corn in flavored oil to coat.

◆ Cook corn on the grill over hot coals 10 to 15 minutes, turning occasionally while cooking. They are ready to serve when they are slightly charred. Serve hot with discs of chili butter.

Vegetables with Herb and Garlic Oil

MAKES 4 TO 6 SERVINGS

4 EARS CORN

8 BABY FENNEL BULBS

4 PLUM TOMATOES

2 RED ONIONS

2 BELL PEPPERS, GREEN, RED OR YELLOW

HERB AND GARLIC OIL

2/3 CUP EXTRA VIRGIN OLIVE OIL

2 TABLESPOONS BALSAMIC VINEGAR

2 GARLIC CLOVES, CRUSHED

2 CUPS CHOPPED FRESH MIXED HERBS (E.G. FENNEL, CHIVES, PARSLEY, BASIL)

SALT AND FRESHLY GROUND BLACK PEPPER

◆ Prepare vegetables for grilling. Peel back husks from corn and knot them at the base. Remove all threads from corn and discard.

◆ Trim baby fennel and halve tomatoes. Halve onions, leaving skins intact. Halve peppers lengthwise and remove cores and seeds, leaving stalks intact.

◆ To make herb and garlic oil, mix together olive oil, balsamic vinegar, garlic and fresh mixed herbs and season to taste with salt and pepper.

◆ Brush vegetables liberally with herb oil and cook on the grill, turning and brushing frequently until they are cooked through and slightly charred. Corn will take about 20 minutes to cook, onions 15 to 20 minutes, and fennel, tomatoes and peppers about 10 minutes.

Spanish Charcoaled Onions

MAKES 8 TO 10 SERVINGS

2 LARGE SPANISH OR RED ONIONS

GARLIC SALT, TO TASTE

¼ CUP HEAVY CREAM, HALF WHIPPED

1 TABLESPOON CRUSHED BLACK PEPPERCORNS

¼ STICK (1 OUNCE) BUTTER

ROSEMARY SPRIGS, TO GARNISH

◆ Peel onions and cut into ½-inch thick slices. Do not separate into rings. Season to taste with garlic salt.

◆ Brush one side with cream and sprinkle with crushed peppercorns. Place in a tented, hinged wire basket.

◆ Grill over hot coals 5 to 8 minutes on each side, cream side up first, until beginning to "charcoal". Place small pieces of butter on surface of onion slices while first sides are cooking.

◆ Serve peppered side up, garnished with sprigs of rosemary.

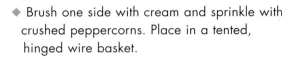

Singed Spiced Plantains

MAKES 6 TO 12 SERVINGS

¼ STICK (1 OUNCE) BUTTER, SOFTENED

2 TABLESPOONS LEMON JUICE

½ TEASPOON QUATRE ÉPICES (SEE NOTE)

DASH GROUND GINGER

6 PLANTAINS (OR UNDER-RIPE BANANAS)

LEMON SLICES, TO GARNISH

Note: Quatre épices is a spicy mixture of ground pepper, cloves, nutmeg and either cinnamon or ginger. It is obtainable from many delicatessens.

◆ Mix lemon juice, quatre épices and ginger into softened butter. Set aside.

◆ Without peeling them, grill plantains over medium coals, turning them over, until skin blackens.

◆ Slice cooked plantains in half lengthwise and spoon juicy butter over the surface. Garnish with lemon slices.

Crusty Garlic Potatoes

1 POUND NEW POTATOES

8 LARGE GARLIC CLOVES

2 EGGS, BEATEN

6 TO 8 TABLESPOONS YELLOW CORNMEAL

PARSLEY LEAVES, TO GARNISH

◆ Scrub potatoes well. Peel garlic, leaving cloves whole. Boil potatoes and garlic in salted water 12 to 15 minutes until just cooked. Drain, reserving garlic.

◆ Skin potatoes as soon as they are cool enough to handle. Roughly chop garlic and, using a small skewer, insert pieces deeply into potatoes.

◆ Dip potatoes first in beaten egg and then in cornmeal. Press on well with a round-bladed knife, then dip in beaten egg once more.

◆ Grill potatoes on a well-oiled grid over hot coals 10 to 15 minutes until crusty and golden.

◆ Serve in a basket lined with a clean cloth and garnish with parsley leaves.

Grilled Eggplant Salad

◆ Cut eggplant into ½-inch slices and onion into ¼-inch slices. Keep onion rings in one piece by inserting 2 cocktail sticks from the outer ring to the center. Place eggplant and onion into a large bowl.

◆ In a small bowl, combine olive oil, red pepper flakes, cumin and sesame seeds, garlic, salt and pepper. Pour mixture over eggplant and onion slices, turning to coat. Marinate at least 30 minutes.

◆ To make dressing, mix together yogurt, cilantro, lime peel, garlic, salt and pepper. Refrigerate until required.

◆ Cook vegetables on a grill rack over hot coals about 5 minutes each side, until slightly blackened. Let cool.

◆ Remove cocktail sticks from onion slices and cut each slice in 4. Cut small eggplant slices in half and larger ones into 4.

◆ Mix onion and eggplant in a serving bowl and sprinkle with lime juice. Carefully fold in yogurt mixture. Let stand at room temperature about 1 hour to allow flavors to develop.

◆ Garnish with lime slices and cilantro leaves. Serve with warm naan bread, if desired.

Sesame-dressed Chicory

◆ To prepare dressing, place olive oil, sesame oil, orange juice, balsamic vinegar, ginger, orange peel, honey, salt and pepper in a screw-top jar and shake vigorously. Refrigerate to let flavors develop.

◆ Wash and dry chicory, brush with dressing and cook on the grill over hot coals about 3 minutes on each side until leaves become lightly charred.

◆ Meanwhile, blanch French beans in boiling water 1 to 2 minutes until tender. Drain, refresh under cold water and pat dry.

◆ Arrange 3 chicory halves on each plate, add beans, drizzle over dressing and sprinkle with sesame seeds. Serve at once.

Spiced Squash

MAKES 4 SERVINGS

*2 SMALL BUTTERNUT SQUASH,
QUARTERED AND SEEDED*

*2 GARLIC CLOVES,
CRUSHED*

2 TEASPOONS GROUND CUMIN

2 TO 3 TABLESPOONS VEGETABLE OIL

JUICE ½ LIME

SALT AND FRESHLY GROUND BLACK PEPPER

◆ Using a small, sharp knife make shallow criss-cross cuts in flesh of each squash quarter.

◆ In a bowl, mix together garlic, cumin, oil and lime juice and season to taste with salt and pepper. Brush over flesh side of each piece of squash, working it well into the cuts.

◆ Cook squash quarters 10 to 15 minutes until they are lightly browned and flesh is tender. Brush occasionally, while cooking, with any remaining cumin mixture.

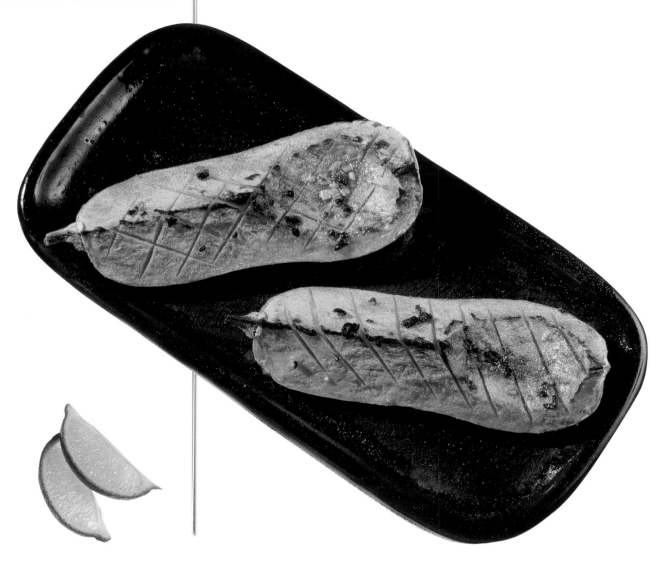

Kabobs

Vegetable Kabobs with Cilantro Sauce

MAKES 4 SERVINGS

2 EARS CORN, SLICED INTO
¾-INCH ROUNDS

2 RED ONIONS, CUT INTO 3-LAYER
1-INCH PIECES

1 RED AND 1 YELLOW BELL PEPPER, SEEDED
AND CUT INTO 1-INCH PIECES

8 BABY PATTYPAN SQUASH, HALVED,
OR 2 SMALL ZUCCHINI, CUT INTO
½-INCH CHUNKS

16 SMALL SHIITAKE MUSHROOMS,
STEMS REMOVED

8 FIRM CHERRY TOMATOES

¾ STICK (3 OUNCES) BUTTER

3 TABLESPOONS OLIVE OIL

1 GARLIC CLOVE,
VERY FINELY CHOPPED

½ TEASPOON CORIANDER SEEDS,
CRUSHED

DASH CAYENNE PEPPER

SALT AND PEPPER

CILANTRO SAUCE

2½ CUPS FRESH, COARSELY
CHOPPED CILANTRO

¾ CUP FRESH, COARSELY CHOPPED
FLAT-LEAF PARSLEY

2 GREEN ONIONS, CHOPPED

1 GARLIC CLOVE, CRUSHED

2 TABLESPOONS LIME JUICE

1½ TEASPOONS TOASTED CUMIN SEEDS

¼ TEASPOON SALT

FRESHLY GROUND BLACK PEPPER, TO TASTE

⅓ CUP PLAIN YOGURT

⅓ CUP HEAVY CREAM

◆ Prepare corn, red onions, peppers, pattypan squash and mushrooms and thread onto 8 skewers with cherry tomatoes. Melt butter with olive oil, garlic, coriander seeds, cayenne pepper and salt and pepper. Brush the kabobs with the melted butter mixture.

◆ To make cilantro sauce, place cilantro, parsley, green onions, garlic, lime juice, cumin seeds, salt and pepper in a food processor and purée 3 minutes, stopping to scrape the sides of the bowl frequently. Pour into a clean bowl and stir in yogurt and cream.

◆ Place kabobs on the grill and cook 15 minutes, turning and basting frequently, until just tender and beginning to blacken around the edges. Serve with cilantro sauce.

Tofu, Leek and Mushroom Saté

◆ Cut tofu into 12 cubes and leeks into 12 thick slices and place in a shallow dish. Wipe mushrooms and add to dish.

◆ To make marinade, mix together soy sauce, garlic, ginger, chile, lime peel and juice, sherry, honey and 3 tablespoons water. Pour over tofu mixture and marinate several hours, stirring occasionally.

◆ To make saté sauce, place ⅔ cup of the marinade into a small pan and add peanut butter and creamed coconut. Heat gently until melted, then stir until thickened.

◆ Thread tofu, leeks and mushrooms onto 8 bamboo skewers and brush with oil. Pour over remaining marinade and place on a prepared grill 10 to 12 minutes, turning and brushing with pan juices, until golden and lightly charred.

◆ Serve with saté sauce as a dip.

Halloumi, Zucchini and Mushroom Skewers

12 OUNCES HALLOUMI CHEESE

1 RED BELL PEPPER,
HALVED, CORED AND SEEDED

1 MEDIUM ZUCCHINI,
CUT INTO 8 CHUNKS

8 LARGE MUSHROOMS, HALVED

½ CUP EXTRA VIRGIN OLIVE OIL

2 TABLESPOONS CHOPPED FRESH THYME

2 GARLIC CLOVES, CHOPPED

FRESHLY GROUND BLACK PEPPER

◆ Cut cheese and red pepper into 1-inch squares. Place them in a shallow dish with zucchini and mushrooms.

◆ In a small bowl, mix together olive oil, thyme, garlic and freshly ground black pepper and pour over vegetables. Toss gently to coat evenly.

◆ Thread cheese and vegetables on skewers, reserving any remaining oil mixture for basting. Cook on the oiled grid of the grill over hot coals about 8 minutes, turning occasionally and brushing with remaining oil mixture.

◆ Skewers are ready to serve when cheese is golden and vegetables are tender.

Spicy Potato, Shallot and Fennel Kabobs

24 (ABOUT 1 POUND)
BABY NEW POTATOES

8 SMALL SHALLOTS

16 (ABOUT 10 OUNCES)
BABY FENNEL BULBS

MARINADE

1 TABLESPOON MUSTARD SEEDS

1 TABLESPOON CUMIN SEEDS

1 TABLESPOON GARAM MASALA

2 TEASPOONS TURMERIC

1 TABLESPOON LEMON JUICE

½ CUP PEANUT OIL

SALT AND FRESHLY GROUND BLACK PEPPER

◆ Cook potatoes in boiling, salted water about 12 minutes until tender. Drain and transfer to a large mixing bowl to cool.

◆ Cook shallots in boiling water 4 minutes, drain and, when cool enough to handle, peel. Add to potatoes, along with fennel bulbs.

◆ To make the marinade, crush mustard and cumin seeds lightly and place them in a bowl with garam masala, turmeric, lemon juice, peanut oil, salt and pepper. Stir to combine.

◆ Pour marinade over prepared vegetables and toss to coat well. Cover and refrigerate 2 hours, if time permits.

◆ Remove vegetables from spicy marinade, reserving any remaining mixture for basting, and thread vegetables onto skewers.

◆ Cook kabobs on the grill about 12 minutes, turning and basting with marinade while cooking.

Eggplant and Mushroom Saté

18 CHESTNUT MUSHROOMS

1 LARGE EGGPLANT (ABOUT 12 OUNCES)

OIL, FOR BRUSHING

CHINESE LEAVES, SHREDDED, TO SERVE

½ SMALL CUCUMBER, CUT INTO MATCHSTICK STRIPS, TO SERVE

2 TABLESPOONS FINELY CHOPPED CILANTRO, TO GARNISH

MARINADE

⅓ CUP OLIVE OIL

3 TABLESPOONS SOY SAUCE

1 TABLESPOON WINE VINEGAR

1 GARLIC CLOVE, CRUSHED

SALT AND FRESHLY GROUND BLACK PEPPER

SATÉ SAUCE

¾ CUP (4 OUNCES) FRESH PEANUTS, ROASTED

2 TEASPOONS CORIANDER SEEDS, ROASTED

2 TEASPOONS VEGETABLE OIL

2 GARLIC CLOVES, FINELY CHOPPED

1 SHALLOT, FINELY CHOPPED

2 TEASPOONS FINELY CHOPPED LEMON GRASS (OR ½ TEASPOON DRIED)

½ TEASPOON CHILI POWDER

1 TEASPOON GROUND CUMIN SEEDS

1 TEASPOON INDONESIAN SOY SAUCE

1 TEASPOON DARK BROWN SUGAR

½ TEASPOON SALT

JUICE ½ LIME OR LEMON

2 TABLESPOONS PLAIN YOGURT

FRESHLY GROUND BLACK PEPPER

◆ Cut mushrooms in half. Cut eggplant into ¾-inch slices then cut each slice into 4 segments. Place vegetables in a shallow dish.

◆ To make the marinade, in a small bowl, mix together olive oil, soy sauce, wine vinegar, garlic, salt and pepper.

◆ Spoon marinade over vegetables, making sure they are thoroughly coated. Leave at least 1 hour, turning occasionally.

◆ To make saté sauce, place peanuts and coriander seeds in a coffee grinder or blender and grind as finely as possible.

◆ Heat oil in a pan. Add garlic, shallot, lemon grass, chili powder and cumin seeds and stir-fry about 1 minute until lightly browned.

◆ Add 2 cups water, soy sauce, dark brown sugar, salt and peanut mixture. Bring to a boil, stirring. Reduce heat and simmer 15 to 20 minutes until thickened, stirring frequently.

◆ Allow to cool slightly, then stir in lime or lemon juice, yogurt and black pepper.

◆ Thread pieces of mushroom and eggplant alternately onto 12 skewers. Brush with oil and place on the grill over hot coals about 10 minutes, turning frequently and brushing with oil, until nicely browned.

◆ Place on a bed of Chinese leaves and cucumber strips. Spoon over some of the saté sauce and serve the rest in a bowl. Sprinkle with cilantro and serve immediately.

Skewered New Potatoes

MAKES 6 SERVINGS

*32 (ABOUT 1½ POUNDS)
BABY NEW POTATOES*

¼ CUP OLIVE OIL

*SEA SALT AND
FRESHLY GROUND BLACK PEPPER*

HERB BUTTER

*¾ STICK (3 OUNCES) BUTTER,
SOFTENED*

*2 TABLESPOONS CHOPPED FRESH HERBS
OF YOUR CHOICE*

SALT AND FRESHLY GROUND BLACK PEPPER

◆ Scrub potatoes and cook them in boiling, salted water about 12 minutes, or until tender. Drain potatoes and, while they are still warm, toss with olive oil and plenty of salt and freshly ground black pepper. Thread 4 potatoes onto each of 8 skewers and set aside until required.

◆ To make herb butter, in a bowl, mix together butter, chopped herbs, salt and pepper. Roll butter into a sausage shape on a piece of waxed paper or plastic wrap. Refrigerate butter until firm enough to slice.

◆ Cook potatoes on the grill over hot coals 12 to 15 minutes, turning frequently. Serve hot with herb butter.

Patty Pan, Onion and Eggplant Kabobs

MAKES 4 SERVINGS

16 SMALL PATTYPAN SQUASH

8 BABY EGGPLANTS, HALVED LENGTHWISE

8 BABY ONIONS, UNPEELED

MARINADE

1/3 CUP CHOPPED FRESH CILANTRO

1/2 CUP OLIVE OIL

1 TEASPOON GARAM MASALA

1 TEASPOON DRIED CHILE FLAKES

2 GARLIC CLOVES, CRUSHED

SALT AND FRESHLY GROUND BLACK PEPPER

◆ To make marinade, mix together in a large bowl chopped cilantro, olive oil, garam masala, dried chile flakes, garlic, salt and pepper.

◆ Boil pattypan squash 4 minutes, drain and add to marinade, along with eggplants.

◆ Boil baby onions 5 minutes, then drain, peel and halve them. Add onions to bowl of vegetables. Toss gently to coat evenly with marinade. Cover and refrigerate 2 hours.

◆ Thread marinated vegetables onto skewers, reserving marinade for basting. Cook kabobs on a prepared grill about 10 minutes, turning and basting occasionally while cooking.

Oriental Tofu Skewers

MAKES 4 SERVINGS

9 OUNCES FIRM TOFU,
CUT INTO 16 CUBES

1 LARGE ORANGE BELL PEPPER

8 CHERRY TOMATOES

8 FLORETS (ABOUT 3 OUNCES) BROCCOLI

SESAME MARINADE

3 TABLESPOONS VEGETABLE OIL

1 TABLESPOON SESAME OIL

1 TABLESPOON SOY SAUCE

1 TEASPOON GRATED FRESH GINGER

1 TEASPOON SESAME SEEDS

2 TABLESPOONS RICE WINE VINEGAR

1 GREEN ONION, FINELY CHOPPED

◆ To make marinade, mix together in a large bowl vegetable oil, sesame oil, soy sauce, ginger, sesame seeds, rice wine vinegar and green onion.

◆ Add tofu cubes to marinade, toss gently to coat, cover and refrigerate 2 hours.

◆ Place pepper on the grill over hot coals and cook, turning frequently, until skin blisters and becomes charred.

◆ Place pepper in a plastic bag and let cool and soften 30 minutes. Peel and discard skin and seeds. Cut flesh into 8 thick slices.

◆ Remove tofu from marinade, reserving remaining marinade for basting. Thread tofu, pepper strips, tomatoes and broccoli on skewers.

◆ Cook skewers on the grill 8 to 10 minutes, turning and basting them while cooking. Just before serving, pour any remaining marinade over tofu skewers.

Mushroom and Mozzarella Brochettes

MAKES 4 SERVINGS

16 FRESH SHIITAKE MUSHROOMS

16 BUTTON MUSHROOMS

16 MINI MOZZARELLA CHEESE BALLS

MARINADE

GRATED PEEL AND JUICE
2 SMALL LEMONS

2 TABLESPOONS OLIVE OIL

2 TEASPOONS CHILI OIL

3 TABLESPOONS CHOPPED
FRESH ROSEMARY

½ SMALL FRESH RED CHILE,
SEEDED AND FINELY CHOPPED

½ SMALL FRESH GREEN CHILE,
SEEDED AND FINELY CHOPPED

2 GARLIC CLOVES, CRUSHED

SALT AND FRESHLY GROUND BLACK PEPPER

◆ To make marinade, mix together in a small bowl lemon peel and juice, olive and chili oils, rosemary, red and green chiles, garlic, salt and freshly ground black pepper.

◆ Place two types of mushrooms and mini mozzarella balls in a mixing bowl. Pour over marinade and toss gently to coat evenly. Cover and refrigerate 2 hours.

◆ Remove marinated mushrooms and cheese from the dish, reserving any remaining marinade for basting, and thread mushrooms and cheese onto skewers. Cook brochettes on a prepared medium-hot grill about 10 minutes, turning and basting them while cooking.

Note: These kabobs taste even better if cooked on rosemary branches rather than on conventional metal skewers.

Hot Hot Aloo

MAKES 4 TO 6 SERVINGS

24 BABY NEW POTATOES
(ABOUT 1 POUND)

¼ CUP LIME PICKLE

¼ CUP OLIVE OIL

2 TEASPOONS TOMATO PASTE

2 TEASPOONS GROUND CARDAMOM

2 TABLESPOONS PLAIN YOGURT

LIME SLICES, TO GARNISH

◆ Wash and scrub potatoes. Cook in salted water until tender but firm. Drain and leave to go cold. Thread onto 4 to 6 skewers.

◆ Place lime pickle in a bowl and, using kitchen scissors, cut up any large pieces of pickle. Blend in oil, tomato paste, cardamom and yogurt. Spoon mixture over skewered potatoes so that each potato is well coated.

◆ Grill potatoes on rack over hot coals about 10 minutes, turning frequently.

◆ Garnish with lime slices and serve immediately.

Mixed Vegetable Kabobs

1 LARGE EGGPLANT (ABOUT 12 OUNCES), CUT INTO BITE-SIZE PIECES

½ LARGE RED BELL PEPPER, SEEDED AND CUT INTO ¾-INCH CUBES

½ LARGE YELLOW BELL PEPPER, SEEDED AND CUT INTO ¾-INCH CUBES

4 SMALL ZUCCHINI, TRIMMED AND CUT INTO ½-INCH SLICES

8 SHALLOTS, QUARTERED

16 BUTTON MUSHROOMS

16 CHERRY TOMATOES

OREGANO AND PARSLEY SPRIGS, TO GARNISH

MARINADE

⅓ CUP OLIVE OIL

1 TABLESPOON RASPBERRY VINEGAR

½ TEASPOON SALT

½ TEASPOON FRESHLY GROUND BLACK PEPPER

1 TEASPOON DRY MUSTARD

1 TABLESPOON LIGHT BROWN SUGAR

1 TABLESPOON CHOPPED FRESH OREGANO

1 TABLESPOON CHOPPED FRESH PARSLEY

◆ To make marinade, mix together in a bowl olive oil, raspberry vinegar, salt, pepper, mustard, light brown sugar, oregano and parsley, stirring until well blended.

◆ Place eggplant in a colander or sieve over a bowl, sprinkle with salt, cover with a plate, weight the top, and leave 30 minutes. Rinse eggplant thoroughly to remove salt, then press out water.

◆ Add eggplant, red and yellow pepper, zucchini, shallots, mushrooms and tomatoes to marinade and turn vegetables carefully to coat completely. Cover with plastic wrap and marinate in the refrigerator 1 hour.

◆ Thread a mixture of vegetables onto skewers. Cook on the grill over hot coals 3 to 5 minutes, brushing with marinade until just tender.

◆ Arrange on a serving dish, garnished with fresh oregano and parsley.

Main Meals

Chicory and Tomato Gratin

4 LARGE PLUMP HEADS CHICORY, HALVED LENGTHWISE

SALT AND FRESHLY GROUND BLACK PEPPER

OLIVE OIL, FOR BRUSHING

2 GARLIC CLOVES, FINELY CHOPPED

⅔ CUP (7 OUNCES) CHOPPED CANNED TOMATOES

2 TEASPOONS FINELY CHOPPED FRESH MARJORAM OR BASIL

⅓ CUP (1½ OUNCES) DRY BREADCRUMBS

½ CUP (1½ OUNCES) FRESHLY GRATED VEGETARIAN PARMESAN

½ STICK (2 OUNCES) BUTTER

◆ Make 2 or 3 deep cuts in the base of chicory heads. With cut side down, place on the grill over hot coals 3 to 5 minutes until just beginning to blacken.

◆ Turn over, sprinkle with salt and freshly ground black pepper and brush generously with olive oil, working oil between leaves.

◆ Cook on the grill, cut side up, 10 to 15 minutes until just tender. Transfer chicory to a shallow dish.

◆ Meanwhile, heat 1 tablespoon olive oil in a small pan. Add garlic and gently fry 30 seconds, then add tomatoes and marjoram or basil. Season to taste with salt and freshly ground black pepper. Simmer 5 minutes, stirring occasionally, then pour mixture over chicory.

◆ Combine breadcrumbs and Parmesan cheese, then sprinkle over chicory. Dot with butter.

◆ Wrap each chicory half tightly in a piece of heavy-duty aluminum foil and place on the grill over hot coals. Cook about 10 minutes, turning half way through cooking time.

Noodles with Marinated Vegetables

2 SMALL RED ONIONS, UNPEELED

2 HEADS PURPLE 'WET' GARLIC

4 SMALL ZUCCHINI

2 SMALL PLUMP HEADS CHICORY

1 EGGPLANT

1 LARGE YELLOW BELL PEPPER, SEEDED

OLIVE OIL, FOR BRUSHING

4 OUNCES EGG VERMICELLI

MARINADE

½ CUP SHREDDED BASIL LEAVES

½ CUP FENNEL FRONDS

½ CUP TRIMMED AND ROUGHLY CHOPPED CILANTRO

1-INCH PIECE FRESH GINGER, FINELY CHOPPED

2 LARGE GARLIC CLOVES, CHOPPED

1 FRESH CHILE, SEEDED AND CHOPPED

FINELY GRATED PEEL AND JUICE 1 LIME

½ CUP OLIVE OIL

½ CUP (2 OUNCES) PEANUTS, TOASTED

1 TEASPOON MUSCOVADO SUGAR

½ TEASPOON SALT

◆ To make marinade, place basil, fennel fronds, cilantro, fresh ginger, garlic, chile, lime peel and juice, olive oil, peanuts, sugar and salt in a blender or food processor and purée until smooth.

◆ Cut red onions and garlic in half crosswise and zucchini and chicory lengthwise. Place vegetables in a single layer in a shallow dish.

◆ Brush vegetables with marinade and drizzle with olive oil. Cover and refrigerate at least 2 hours, preferably overnight.

◆ Remove vegetables, scraping off and reserving marinade, and place on the grill over medium-hot coals. Grill 10 to 15 minutes, brushing with oil and turning occasionally, until tender and beginning to blacken.

◆ Meanwhile, cook vermicelli, following package directions. Drain, return to the pan and toss with reserved marinade.

◆ Arrange a nest of vermicelli on 4 plates and top with a selection of grilled vegetables.

Savoy Cabbage Packages

4 LARGE SAVOY OR POINTED GREEN
CABBAGE LEAVES

¾ STICK (3 OUNCES) BUTTER

1 SMALL LEEK, THINLY SLICED

1 LARGE CARROT,
PEELED AND COARSELY GRATED

2⅔ CUPS (6 OUNCES) COOKED
BROWN BASMATI RICE

¼ CUP (1 OUNCE) PUMPKIN SEEDS,
LIGHTLY TOASTED

2 TABLESPOONS CHOPPED
FRESH TARRAGON

SALT AND FRESHLY GROUND BLACK PEPPER

◆ Cut away tough stalks from cabbage leaves, then blanch leaves in boiling, salted water 1 to 2 minutes until they are just tender. Drain and refresh in cold water, then dry cabbage leaves on paper towels.

◆ Melt 2 ounces (½ stick) of butter in a pan, add leeks and cook and stir them 3 minutes. Stir in carrot and cook, stirring, one more minute. Remove pan from heat and stir in rice, pumpkin seeds, tarragon and seasoning.

◆ Lay a cabbage leaf on a large piece of heavy-duty aluminum foil and place one quarter of rice mixture in the center. Fold cabbage around filling to form a package, dot with one quarter of remaining butter and fold up foil to enclose cabbage. Repeat with remaining leaves and filling.

◆ Cook foil packages on the grill 13 to 15 minutes, until cabbage is tender and filling is heated through.

Bell Peppers Stuffed with Nutty Rice

1 CUP (8 OUNCES) BASMATI RICE

1 TEASPOON SAFFRON STRANDS

¼ CUP VEGETABLE OIL

1 RED ONION, THINLY SLICED

4 SMALL GARLIC CLOVES, CRUSHED

½ CUP (2 OUNCES) PINE NUTS, TOASTED

⅓ CUP (1 OUNCE) SHELLED AND CHOPPED
PISTACHIO NUTS

¼ CUP CHOPPED FRESH PARSLEY

SALT AND FRESHLY GROUND BLACK PEPPER

4 MEDIUM RED BELL PEPPERS

OIL, FOR BRUSHING

◆ Infuse saffron threads in 3 tablespoons boiling water 10 minutes. Add saffron and its water to pan of boiling, salted water with basmati rice. Bring back to simmer and cook 10 minutes. Drain rice and place in a mixing bowl.

◆ Heat oil in a pan and stir and cook onion and garlic 2 to 3 minutes. Add to rice, with pine nuts, pistachios, parsley and seasoning. Toss to combine.

◆ Halve bell peppers lengthwise and core and seed, leaving stalks intact. Divide nutty rice between pepper halves.

◆ Lightly oil 4 large pieces heavy-duty aluminum foil and place 2 bell pepper halves on each piece of foil. Fold foil over to enclose fillings.

◆ Cook on a prepared grill about 20 minutes, until peppers are tender and rice is hot.

Grilled Vegetable Pizza

1 READY-MADE PIZZA CRUST

TOPPING

1 RED BELL PEPPER, QUARTERED AND SEEDED

1 SMALL ZUCCHINI, SLICED

1 SMALL EGGPLANT, SLICED

1 SMALL ONION, THINLY SLICED

*6 LARGE RIPE TOMATOES,
HALVED AND SEEDED*

2 TABLESPOONS PESTO SAUCE

SALT AND FRESHLY GROUND BLACK PEPPER

*1 HEAPED CUP (5 OUNCES) SHREDDED
MOZZARELLA CHEESE*

◆ Preheat oven to 450°F and place a pizza plate or baking sheet on the top shelf.

◆ Brush bell peppers, zucchini, eggplant and onion slices with a little oil and place on the grill over hot coals until charred all over.

◆ Place tomato halves skin side up on the grill rack and cook until blistered. Peel and discard skin and mash flesh with pesto sauce and salt and pepper.

◆ Spread tomato mixture over pizza crust and arrange grilled vegetables over the top. Sprinkle over shredded mozzarella cheese and transfer to hot pizza plate or baking sheet.

◆ Bake pizza in oven 25 to 30 minutes until bubbling and golden.

Falafel Patties with Yogurt and Mint Dip

MAKES 4 SERVINGS

2 TABLESPOONS VEGETABLE OIL

1 TEASPOON CUMIN SEEDS

1 ONION, FINELY CHOPPED

2 GARLIC CLOVES, CRUSHED

1 TEASPOON CHOPPED
FRESH GREEN CHILE

½ TEASPOON TURMERIC

ONE 15-OUNCE CAN
GARBANZO BEANS, DRAINED

SALT AND FRESHLY GROUND
BLACK PEPPER

½ CUP (2 OUNCES) FRESH
WHITE BREADCRUMBS

1 EGG, BEATEN

2 TABLESPOONS CHOPPED
FRESH CILANTRO

FLOUR, FOR COATING

OIL, FOR BRUSHING

LEMON WEDGES, TO SERVE

PITA BREAD, TO SERVE

YOGURT AND MINT DIP

½ CUP PLAIN YOGURT

¼ CUP CHOPPED FRESH MINT

1 TEASPOON LEMON JUICE

DASH GROUND CUMIN

SALT AND FRESHLY GROUND
BLACK PEPPER

◆ To make dip, in a bowl, mix together yogurt, mint, lemon juice, cumin and seasoning. Cover and refrigerate until required.

◆ Heat vegetable oil in a skillet, add cumin seeds, onion and garlic and stir-fry 5 minutes. Add chile and turmeric and cook 2 more minutes.

◆ Transfer spice mixture to a blender or food processor, add garbanzo beans and seasoning, and blend or process briefly until garbanzo beans are roughly mashed and combined with spices.

◆ Transfer to a bowl and add breadcrumbs, beaten egg and cilantro. Mix to combine and divide into 8 portions. With floured hands, shape into patties and refrigerate these falafel about 4 hours.

◆ Brush falafel all over with oil. Place on an oiled griddle plate, or in a wire basket, and cook on the grill 6 to 7 minutes on each side.

◆ Serve hot with dip, lemon wedges and pita bread.

Eggplant Layers

2 LARGE EGGPLANTS

1 TEASPOON SALT

2 RED BELL PEPPERS

⅓ CUP OLIVE OIL

10 OUNCES MOZZARELLA CHEESE, THINLY SLICED

OREGANO LEAVES, TO GARNISH

TOMATO SAUCE

2 TABLESPOONS OLIVE OIL

2 GARLIC CLOVES, CRUSHED

5 (1½ POUNDS) PLUM TOMATOES, PEELED, SEEDED AND CHOPPED (SEE NOTE)

2 TEASPOONS CHOPPED FRESH OREGANO

SALT AND FRESHLY GROUND BLACK PEPPER

Note: To peel tomatoes, make slits in the skin, place in boiling water a minute or two, refresh in cold water, then peel away skins.

◆ Cut eggplants into 1½-inch thick slices. Place in a colander, sprinkle with salt and leave 1 hour.

◆ Place bell peppers on the grill over hot coals until skins are beginning to blacken. Place into a plastic bag a few minutes while still hot. Remove from plastic bag, peel and cut into thin strips.

◆ To make tomato sauce, heat olive oil in a pan. Add garlic and cook, stirring, a few minutes until soft. Add tomatoes, oregano, salt and pepper and cook gently, stirring, 2 minutes, without allowing tomatoes to lose their texture. Remove from heat and keep warm.

◆ Rinse eggplants well, drain and dry thoroughly with paper towels. Brush with ¼ cup olive oil, place on grill and cook on both sides until soft and beginning to brown.

◆ Place half the eggplant slices onto a baking sheet or plate. Arrange mozzarella slices on top, cutting to fit if necessary. Top with half the bell pepper strips. Place remaining eggplant slices on top. Drizzle remaining olive oil over eggplant.

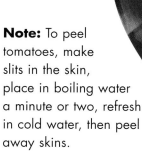

◆ Place in a hinged wire basket and grill over hot coals about 2 minutes on each side until heated through, but do not allow mozzarella to melt.

◆ Remove from the wire basket onto serving plates, arrange remaining strips of bell pepper on top, garnish with oregano leaves and serve with tomato sauce.

Stuffed Eggplants

MAKES 6 SERVINGS

6 SMALL EGGPLANTS,
(EACH WEIGHING ABOUT 6 OUNCES)

¼ STICK (1 OUNCE) BUTTER

1 ONION, FINELY CHOPPED

1 GARLIC CLOVE, CRUSHED

1 CUP (8 OUNCES) CHOPPED
CANNED TOMATOES

1¼ CUPS (3 OUNCES) FRESH
BREADCRUMBS

½ CUP (2 OUNCES) SHREDDED
VEGETARIAN CHEDDAR CHEESE

1 TEASPOON DRIED OREGANO

SALT AND FRESHLY GROUND BLACK PEPPER

OREGANO SPRIGS, TO GARNISH

◆ Cut off a thin slice along the length of each eggplant and reserve. Scoop out flesh from eggplants, leaving a ¼-inch wall. Finely chop reserved flesh.

◆ Melt butter in a pan and gently fry onion and garlic until soft. Add chopped eggplant and continue cooking, stirring, until tender.

◆ Remove from heat and stir in tomatoes, breadcrumbs, cheese and oregano. Season to taste with salt and freshly ground black pepper.

◆ Pack filling into eggplant shells. Replace lids and wrap separately in squares of lightly oiled, double-thickness aluminum foil.

◆ Place on the grid over medium coals, or cook directly in coals, 20 to 30 minutes.

◆ Garnish with sprigs of oregano and serve.

Potato and Egg Bell Peppers

MAKES 4 SERVINGS

4 SMALL GREEN BELL PEPPERS

4 HARD-BOILED EGGS,
SHELLED

1 CUP (8 OUNCES) COOKED AND
DICED POTATO

3 TABLESPOONS MAYONNAISE

2 TEASPOONS FRENCH MUSTARD

1 ROUNDED TABLESPOON
CHOPPED FRESH CHIVES

1 TEASPOON PAPRIKA

½ TEASPOON GARLIC SALT

FRESHLY GROUND BLACK PEPPER

PARSLEY SPRIGS, TO GARNISH

◆ Cut away a thin slice from stalk end of each bell pepper. Remove core, seeds and pith.

◆ In a mixing bowl, coarsely chop hard-cooked eggs and stir in cooked, diced potato. Add mayonnaise, mustard, chives, paprika, garlic salt and black pepper to taste. Mix well. Carefully spoon mixture into peppers.

◆ Wrap each pepper separately in lightly buttered, double-thickness aluminum foil and cook on the grid, or directly in coals, about 30 minutes until peppers are tender, turning packages over occasionally. Garnish with sprigs of parsley.

Brazil Nut Burgers

MAKES 6 SERVINGS

3 TABLESPOONS (1½ OUNCES) BUTTER

1 ONION, FINELY CHOPPED

1 CELERY STALK, FINELY CHOPPED

½ SMALL GREEN BELL PEPPER,
SEEDED AND CHOPPED

1½ CUPS (8 OUNCES) SHELLED
BRAZIL NUTS, GROUND

1 CARROT, GRATED

1 TEASPOON YEAST EXTRACT

1 CUP VEGETABLE STOCK

⅓ CUP (2 OUNCES) BULGUR

SALT AND FRESHLY GROUND BLACK PEPPER

2 EGGS, BEATEN

FLOUR, FOR DUSTING

½ SMALL GREEN BELL PEPPER, SLICED INTO 6
RINGS, TO GARNISH

◆ In a heavy-bottomed pan, melt butter and fry onion, celery and pepper until soft. Stir in Brazil nuts and cook 3 to 4 minutes, stirring continually to bring out the flavor.

◆ Stir grated carrot, yeast extract and vegetable stock into mixture and bring to a boil, then simmer 5 minutes. Mix in bulgur and season to taste with salt and freshly ground black pepper. Let cool.

◆ Bind mixture together with beaten eggs to the consistency of thick paste. Shape into 6 burgers and dust with flour. Place burgers on a well-oiled griddle pan.

◆ Place on the grill and cook over hot coals 10 minutes, turning burgers once during cooking. Carefully remove burgers from grill and garnish with green pepper rings.

Green Lentil Zucchini

MAKES 4 SERVINGS

3 LARGE FIRM ZUCCHINI

2 GREEN ONIONS, FINELY CHOPPED

1 SMALL GREEN BELL PEPPER, FINELY CHOPPED

1 TOMATO, PEELED AND CHOPPED

1¼ CUPS (4 OUNCES) COOKED
GREEN LENTILS

1 TEASPOON FRESH BASIL LEAVES, CHOPPED,
AND WHOLE LEAVES, FOR GARNISHING

SALT AND FRESHLY GROUND BLACK PEPPER

¼ CUP GRATED, ROASTED HAZELNUTS

◆ Halve zucchini lengthwise. Scoop pulp into a bowl, leaving ¼-inch thick shells to prevent zucchini from collapsing. Reserve shells.

◆ Add green onion, pepper and tomato to zucchini pulp and mix in lentils and basil. Season to taste. Pile mixture high into reserved shells.

◆ Place zucchini halves individually onto large squares of double-thickness aluminum foil. Wrap up securely, leaving a space above stuffing for steam to circulate.

◆ Grill over hot coals about 20 minutes until zucchini are tender but firm. Open packages and sprinkle hazelnuts over stuffing. Garnish with sprigs of basil to serve.

Grilled Tomato and Asparagus Salad

12 THICK ASPARAGUS SPEARS, TRIMMED

EXTRA VIRGIN OLIVE OIL, FOR BRUSHING

*8 RIPE PLUM TOMATOES,
QUARTERED AND SEEDED*

⅓ CUP (2 OUNCES) BABY SPINACH LEAVES

6 OUNCES MOZZARELLA CHEESE, SLICED

8 RIPE OLIVES

1 CUP PESTO

EXTRA VIRGIN OLIVE OIL, FOR DRESSING

◆ Slice asparagus spears in half and brush with a little oil. Place in a wire basket, or directly onto the grill, and cook about 6 minutes, turning frequently, until charred and tender. Let cool.

◆ Drizzle a little oil over tomato quarters and grill 2 to 3 minutes until just softened. Let cool, then peel away and discard skins.

◆ Arrange asparagus and tomatoes on plates. Add spinach leaves, mozzarella slices and olives.

◆ Mix pesto with extra virgin olive oil to make a dressing and drizzle over salad. Serve immediately.

Stuffed Onions with Sun-dried Tomatoes

MAKES 2 SERVINGS

3 LARGE ONIONS, UNPEELED

1 CUP (4 OUNCES) DRAINED SUN-DRIED TOMATOES IN OIL, THINLY SLICED

4 OUNCES GOAT'S CHEESE, CUBED

1 GARLIC CLOVE, CRUSHED

½ CUP (2 OUNCES) FRESH WHITE BREADCRUMBS

¼ CUP (1 OUNCE) PINE NUTS, TOASTED

1 TABLESPOON CHOPPED FRESH BASIL

1 TEASPOON CHOPPED FRESH THYME

1 EGG

SALT AND FRESHLY GROUND BLACK PEPPER

◆ Place unpeeled onions in a large pan and cover with cold water. Bring to a boil and cook 15 minutes, until tender. Drain onions and let cool.

◆ Place tomatoes, cheese, garlic, breadcrumbs, pine nuts, basil and thyme in a large bowl and mix together.

◆ Cut cooled onions in half, through the root and tip, and carefully cut out most of the flesh, leaving 1 or 2 layers to keep the shape and form the empty shells.

◆ Discard half the flesh, finely chop the rest, and stir into reserved filling. Lightly beat egg and stir into filling.

◆ Place each onion half on a large square of double-thickness aluminum foil. Spoon filling into empty shells, packing the mixture in well. Fold foil over filling and secure.

◆ Cook on the grill over hot coals about 20 to 25 minutes, or directly in coals about 15 minutes.

◆ Serve hot, warm or cold.

Note: This dish also makes an ideal appetizer, in which case it will make 6 servings.

Fruit

Kiwis and Candied Ginger

◆ Rinse and dry kiwi fruit and halve lengthwise. Remove firm cores, chop and reserve. Spoon a little ginger syrup over kiwi flesh and pierce with a skewer to help absorption.

◆ In a bowl, stiffly whip cream with confectioners' sugar and refrigerate.

◆ Place pieces of candied ginger in cavities in kiwi fruit. Place each filled kiwi half, skin side down, onto a square of heavy-duty aluminum foil and pour a little more ginger syrup over. Wrap up securely.

◆ Grill packages over medium-hot coals 10 to 15 minutes, turning over towards end of cooking time.

◆ Open packages and sprinkle cut surfaces of fruit with nuts and reserved chopped cores. Serve with sweetened whipped cream.

Spiced Fruit Kabobs

◆ Soak about 20 bamboo skewers in water 30 minutes.

◆ Cut fruit into bite-size chunks. Thread a selection of pieces of fruit onto each skewer.

◆ Melt butter and stir in grated fresh ginger, confectioners' sugar and lime juice. Brush over kabobs.

◆ Cook kabobs on the grill, over medium coals, turning frequently and brushing with butter mixture, about 5 minutes, or until beginning to caramelize.

Baked Demelza Apples

2½ TABLESPOONS (1 OUNCE) RAISINS

2½ TABLESPOONS (1 OUNCE) GOLDEN RAISINS

⅓ CUP GINGER WINE, MADEIRA OR SWEET SHERRY

¾ CUP (3 OUNCES) SLIVERED ALMONDS, TOASTED

1 TO 2 TABLESPOONS MARMALADE

4 LARGE COOKING APPLES

CHILLED WHIPPED CREAM, TO SERVE

◆ Place raisins and golden raisins into a small bowl and add ginger wine, Madeira or sherry. Let soak several hours.

◆ Drain raisins, reserving liquid, and place in a bowl. Add slivered almonds and marmalade and stir to combine.

◆ Wash and dry apples, but do not peel. Remove core using an apple corer and score a line around each apple. Stand each apple on a piece of double-thickness aluminum foil.

◆ Fill apple cavities with dried fruit mixture, pushing it down firmly. Fold up edges of foil, leaving a gap at the top, and pour strained liquid over apples.

◆ Place apple packages on a rack over medium coals 45 to 50 minutes, turning occasionally, until soft. Alternatively, cook packages directly in the coals 20 to 30 minutes.

◆ Remove apples from foil, place on serving dishes, and pile a spoonful of whipped cream on top of each apple to serve.

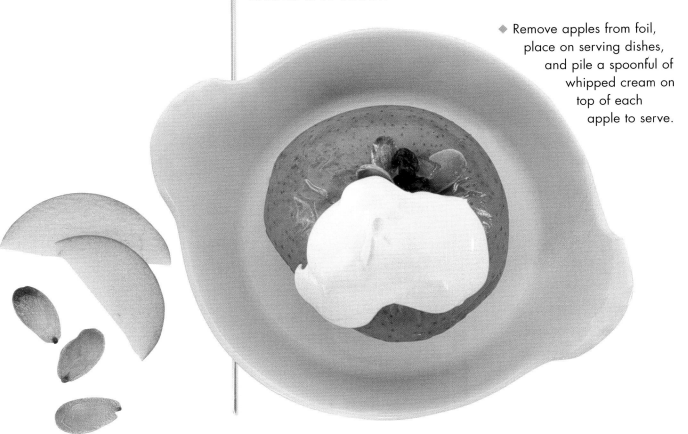

Caribbean Fruit Kabobs with Honey Glaze

*1 SMALL MANGO,
PEELED AND PITTED*

*½ SMALL PINEAPPLE, CUT
LENGTHWISE AND PEELED*

2 SMALL DESERT APPLES

*2 LARGE BANANAS,
PEELED*

24 KUMQUATS

GLAZE

⅔ CUP CLEAR HONEY

GRATED PEEL AND JUICE 1 ORANGE

¼ TEASPOON GROUND CLOVES

◆ Cut mango flesh into 12 chunks. Halve pineapple, remove center core, and cut each ¼ into 6 slices. Cut apples into 12 wedges, cut bananas into 12 thick slices, and wash and dry kumquats.

◆ Thread 2 kumquats and 1 piece each of the other prepared fruits onto each of 12 skewers. Place in a large shallow dish.

◆ To make the glaze, blend together honey, orange peel and juice and ground cloves and pour over kabobs. Cover and marinate 30 minutes, turning once.

◆ Cook kabobs on the grill over hot coals 6 to 8 minutes, turning and basting frequently with glaze, until fruit is lightly browned and sizzling. Serve hot.

Foiled Rum Bananas

MAKES 6 SERVINGS

6 BANANAS, PEELED

2 TABLESPOONS CHOPPED CANDIED GINGER

2 TABLESPOONS CANDIED GINGER SYRUP

¼ CUP DARK RUM

2 TABLESPOONS ORANGE JUICE

¼ STICK (1 OUNCE) BUTTER

*CREAM OR PLAIN YOGURT,
TO SERVE*

◆ Cut each banana in half lengthwise and place in the center of a double layer of aluminum foil. Pull edges up, leaving a small gap at the top.

◆ Add 1 teaspoon chopped candied ginger, 1 teaspoon syrup, 2 teaspoons rum, 1 teaspoon orange juice and 1 teaspoon butter to each package.

◆ Turn edges of foil over to seal well and cook on the grill over hot coals 5 to 6 minutes until bananas are succulent and tender.

◆ Serve immediately with cream or yogurt.

Figs with Cinnamon Cream

MAKES 6 SERVINGS

9 LARGE RIPE FIGS

½ STICK (2 OUNCES) BUTTER

4 TEASPOONS BRANDY

3 TEASPOONS BROWN SUGAR

SLIVERED ALMONDS, TO DECORATE

CINNAMON CREAM

⅔ CUP HEAVY CREAM

1 TEASPOON GROUND CINNAMON

1 TABLESPOON BRANDY

2 TEASPOONS CLEAR HONEY

◆ To make cinnamon cream, in a small bowl, combine cream, ground cinnamon, brandy and honey. Cover and refrigerate 30 minutes to allow tflavors to develop.

◆ Halve figs and thread onto 6 skewers. Melt butter in a small pan and stir in brandy. Brush figs with brandy butter and sprinkle with a little sugar.

◆ Place kabobs on the grill over medium coals 4 to 5 minutes until bubbling and golden.

◆ Whip cinnamon cream until just holding its shape and serve with grilled figs, decorated with slivered almonds.

Hot Tropicanas

MAKES 6 SERVINGS

3 PINK GRAPEFRUIT

8 LYCHEES

*2 KUMQUATS,
RINSED AND DRIED*

1 GUAVA

1 PAPAYA

1 SMALL MANGO

¼ CUP LIGHT CORN SYRUP

¼ STICK (1 OUNCE) BUTTER

*2 TABLESPOONS DRIED COCONUT,
TOASTED (SEE BELOW)*

*MINT SPRIGS,
TO GARNISH*

◆ Halve grapefruit, separate and remove segments to a large mixing bowl, and drain shells. Scrape out grapefruit shells, discarding membranes.

◆ Peel and pit lychees. Slice kumquats. Halve guava and papaya, scoop out seeds, then peel and dice flesh. Peel mango, pare flesh away from pit and cut into strips. Combine all fruits in bowl with grapefruit.

◆ Melt corn syrup, pour over fruits and mix gently. Spoon into grapefruit shells. Top each with 1 teaspoon butter.

◆ Wrap grapefruit shells in large individual pieces of double-thickness aluminum foil and grill over medium coals 7 to 10 minutes until fruit is warm but not cooked.

◆ Remove grapefruit from foil, place in individual dishes, top with toasted coconut and garnish with sprigs of mint.

Coconut Pineapple

MAKES 4 SERVINGS

¼ CUP DRIED COCONUT

1 PINEAPPLE

2 TABLESPOONS RUM

*¼ CUP FIRMLY PACKED (2 OUNCES)
BROWN SUGAR*

◆ Line a broiler pan with aluminium foil and spread coconut over. Broil under low heat, stirring frequently, until beginning to brown. Set aside.

◆ Using a sharp knife, cut pineapple, lengthwise, into 8 wedges, cutting through leaves and leaving them attached to the pineapple wedges. Cut away core. Sprinkle rum, then brown sugar, evenly over pineapple flesh.

◆ Place pineapple wedges on the grill over medium coals until sugar begins to caramelize and pineapple is hot and beginning to soften.

◆ Sprinkle over reserved toasted coconut to serve.

Bananas with Maple Syrup and Pecan Nuts

MAKES 4 SERVINGS

½ CUP (2 OUNCES) COARSELY CHOPPED
PECAN NUTS

⅓ CUP MAPLE SYRUP

4 BANANAS

VANILLA OR RUM AND RAISIN ICE CREAM,
TO SERVE (OPTIONAL)

◆ Cook whole bananas in their skins on the grill 12 to 15 minutes, until skins are completely black and bananas are soft.

◆ Just before serving, gently warm pecan nuts and maple syrup in a pan over low heat.

◆ To serve, remove bananas from their skins and top with warm nutty syrup and scoops of ice cream, if desired.

Fruit Skewers with Chocolate Nut Sauce

MAKES 6 SERVINGS

12 STRAWBERRIES

6 APRICOTS, HALVED

3 PEARS, PEELED AND
CUT INTO QUARTERS

2 TABLESPOONS SUPERFINE SUGAR

CHOCOLATE NUT SAUCE

4 OUNCES MILK CHOCOLATE,
CHOPPED

⅔ CUP LIGHT CREAM

6 MARSHMALLOWS,
CHOPPED

¼ CUP (1 OUNCE) SKINLESS HAZELNUTS,
TOASTED AND CHOPPED

◆ To make sauce, melt chocolate, cream and marshmallows in a pan over low heat, stirring continually.

◆ Whisk to produce a smooth sauce and boil 2 minutes to thicken. Stir in nuts and set sauce aside.

◆ Place strawberries, apricots and pears in a bowl, sprinkle over sugar and toss gently to coat. Divide fruit between skewers.

◆ Place fruit skewers on the grill and cook them 5 to 6 minutes, turning frequently, until fruit is warmed through.

◆ Serve hot with chocolate nut sauce passed separately for dipping.

Walnut Apple Crescents

MAKES 4 SERVINGS

¼ CUP APPLE JUICE

1 TEASPOON GRATED ORANGE PEEL

*¼ CUP (1 OUNCE) SHELLED WALNUTS,
ROUGHLY CHOPPED*

*2 TABLESPOONS (1 OUNCE)
PITTED AND CHOPPED DATES*

2 SMALL RED-SKINNED EATING APPLES

*STRIPS ORANGE PEEL,
TO GARNISH*

◆ Place apple juice and grated orange peel in a small pan. Add walnuts and dates, bring to a boil, then simmer 2 to 3 minutes until liquid has been absorbed. Cool slightly.

◆ Rinse and dry apples and remove core, keeping apples whole. Cut each apple in half lengthwise. (Each half will have a tubular-shaped hollow along its center.)

◆ Fill apple hollows with fruit and nut mixture and wrap each apple half in double-thickness aluminum foil.

◆ Grill over hot coals about 30 minutes, turning occasionally, until apples are tender. Garnish with strips of orange peel to serve.

Rum and Raisin Persimmon

MAKES 6 SERVINGS

6 FIRM PERSIMMON

*2½ TABLESPOONS (1 OUNCE)
MIXED DRIED FRUIT*

1 CANDIED CHERRY

3 UNSKINNED ALMONDS

2 TEASPOONS DARK BROWN SUGAR

1 TEASPOON DARK RUM

DASH GROUND CINNAMON

½ TEASPOON LEMON JUICE

*6 SMALL STRAWBERRIES,
TO GARNISH*

◆ Remove stalks from persimmon and, using a teaspoon, scoop out pulp, leaving fleshy wall intact. Place pulp in a bowl.

◆ Using a sharp, lightly floured knife, very finely chop dried fruit, candied cherry and almonds. Mix into sharon fruit pulp, adding sugar, rum, cinnamon and lemon juice and stirring to combine.

◆ Carefully pack filling into sharon fruit shells and wrap each one separately in a piece of lightly oiled, double-thickness aluminum foil.

◆ Place foil packages in medium coals and cook 25 to 30 minutes until fruit is soft.

◆ To serve, unwrap parcels and top each one with a strawberry.

Praline Bananas

6 UNDER-RIPE BANANAS

*WHIPPED CREAM,
TO SERVE*

PRALINE

*1 TABLESPOON (½ OUNCE)
UNSKINNED ALMONDS*

*1 TABLESPOON (½ OUNCE)
UNSKINNED HAZELNUTS*

¼ CUP (2 OUNCES) GRANULATED SUGAR

◆ To make the praline, place almonds, hazelnuts and sugar in a small, heavy-bottomed skillet. Heat gently, stirring continually, until sugar dissolves. Raise heat and cook to a deep brown syrup.

◆ Immediately, pour this toffee-like mixture onto a sheet of non-stick baking parchment placed on a metal baking sheet on a wooden board. (It will be very hot.) Leave until cold and brittle, then crush finely.

◆ Lay unpeeled bananas flat and make a slit through the skin lengthwise. Slightly open out the skin and fill each banana with about 3 teaspoons of praline.

◆ Re-shape bananas and wrap individually and tightly in double-thickness aluminum foil, sealing along the top.

◆ Grill banana packages directly on medium coals 8 to 10 minutes, turning them over halfway through cooking time.

◆ To serve, unfold foil wrapping and slightly open banana skins. Serve with whipped cream.

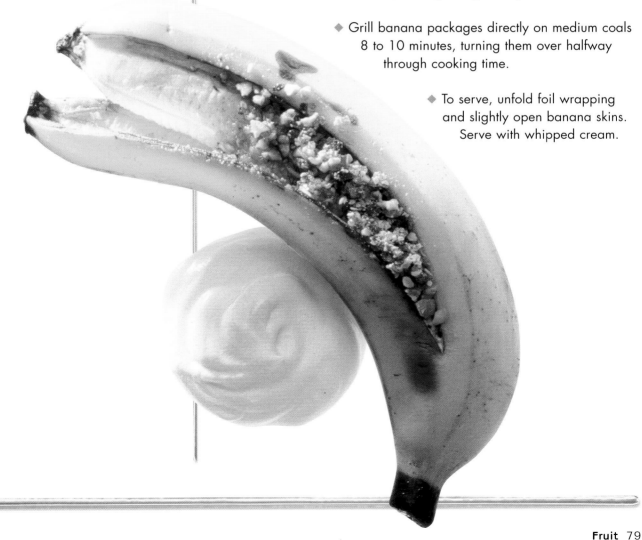

Exotic Fruit with Passion Fruit Dip

1 SMALL RIPE PAPAYA

1 SMALL RIPE MANGO

2 BANANAS

2 THICK SLICES FRESH PINEAPPLE, HALVED

½ STICK (2 OUNCES) BUTTER, MELTED

2 TEASPOONS CONFECTIONERS' SUGAR, SIFTED

PASSION FRUIT DIP

1 CUP THICK SOUR CREAM

1 TABLESPOON CONFECTIONERS' SUGAR, SIFTED

PULP AND JUICE 3 PASSION FRUIT

MINT SPRIGS, TO DECORATE

◆ To make dip, mix together in a bowl thick sour cream, confectioners' sugar and passion fruit pulp and juice. Cover and refrigerate until required.

◆ Cut the papaya into 4 thick slices and seed. Cut the mango into quarters around the pit. Halve the bananas lengthwise, but do not peel.

◆ Place papaya and pineapple slices, mango quarters and banana halves on a large tray. Mix together melted butter and confectioners' sugar, and brush mixture all over fruit.

◆ Cook all fruit on the grill, turning papaya, mango and pineapple over occasionally until they begin to caramelize. The papaya will take about 4 minutes to cook and the mango, pineapple and bananas about 6.

◆ Garnish with mint sprigs and serve fruit with dip.

Peach and Almond Dessert with Amaretto

1 CUP (2 OUNCES) MADIERA CAKE CRUMBS

6 AMARETTI BISCUITS, COARSELY CRUSHED

¼ CUP AMARETTO LIQUEUR

4 RIPE PEACHES, HALVED AND PITTED

¼ CUP (1 OUNCE) SLIVERED ALMONDS, TOASTED

½ CUP FRESHLY SQUEEZED ORANGE JUICE

MASCARPONE CHEESE, TO SERVE

◆ Mix cake crumbs, amaretti biscuits and 2 tablespoons of Amaretto liqueur together in a bowl.

◆ Divide mixture between hollows of peaches. Sprinkle a few slivered almonds onto each peach half.

◆ Mix together remaining Amaretto liqueur and orange juice. Place 2 peach halves on a large piece of double-thickness aluminum foil. Spoon one quarter of the orange juice mixture over each peach half and fold over foil to make a package. Repeat with remaining peaches.

◆ Cook peach packages on the grill about 10 minutes, until they are tender and warmed through. Serve with Mascarpone cheese.

Grand Marnier Kabobs

3 FIRM APRICOTS

3 FIRM FRESH FIGS

2 PINEAPPLE SLICES,
EACH 1 INCH THICK

2/3 CUP (6 OUNCES) CANNED
MANDARIN ORANGES

2 FIRM BANANAS

2 EATING APPLES

1 TABLESPOON LEMON JUICE

3/4 STICK (3 OUNCES) BUTTER

3/4 CUP (3 OUNCES)
CONFECTIONERS' SUGAR

1 TABLESPOON GRAND MARNIER

1 TABLESPOON FRESH ORANGE JUICE

1 TABLESPOON FINELY GRATED
ORANGE PEEL

◆ Halve apricots and remove pits. Remove stalks from figs and quarter lengthwise. Remove and discard any woody core from pineapple slices, trim, and cut pineapple slices into chunks.

◆ Peel satsumas and quarter, but do not remove membranes. Peel bananas and cut into 1-inch-thick slices. Peel apples, cut into quarters, remove cores and halve each apple piece crosswise. Sprinkle apples and bananas with lemon juice to prevent discoloration.

◆ Thread fruit onto 6 to 8 skewers, making sure that each has a mixture of fruit and starting and finishing with apple and pineapple.

◆ Melt butter, stir in confectioners' sugar, then add Grand Marnier, orange juice and peel. Brush kabobs with sauce.

◆ Grill over medium coals 5 to 6 minutes, frequently basting with sauce. Serve kabobs hot with any remaining sauce.

Peaches and Butterscotch

6 PEACHES,
HALVED AND STONED

¾ CUP (2 OUNCES) GROUND ALMONDS

3 TABLESPOONS FINELY CHOPPED
ANGELICA

BUTTERSCOTCH SAUCE

½ CUP FIRMLY PACKED (3 OUNCES)
LIGHT BROWN SUGAR

⅔ CUP MAPLE SYRUP

3 TABLESPOONS (1½ OUNCES)
BUTTER

DASH SALT

⅔ CUP LIGHT CREAM

FEW DROPS VANILLA EXTRACT

◆ To make butterscotch sauce, combine brown sugar, maple syrup, butter and salt in a heavy-bottomed pan. Bring to a boil, stir once, then boil 3 minutes to form a thick syrup.

◆ Stir in cream, bring back to a boil and immediately remove from heat. Stir in vanilla extract to taste. Pour into a jug and keep warm.

◆ Place peach halves, cut sides down, on individual squares of double-thickness aluminum foil. Curl up sides of foil, but do not seal. Grill over hot coals 5 minutes.

◆ Turn peaches over on foil, spoon almonds and 2 tablespoons angelica into cavities and pour 1 tablespoon butterscotch sauce over each one. Draw up edges of foil and twist above peaches to seal. Grill 10 minutes until tender.

◆ Decorate with remaining angelica and serve hot with remaining sauce.

Vodka-soused Pineapple

4 LARGE, FRESH PINEAPPLE SLICES,
EACH 1 INCH THICK

3 TABLESPOONS VODKA

¾ STICK (3 OUNCES) BUTTER

¼ CUP HEAVY CREAM

1 TEASPOON GROUND CARDAMOM

2 TABLESPOONS CONFECTIONERS' SUGAR

12 BOTTLED MORELLO CHERRIES

CONFECTIONERS' SUGAR, FOR DUSTING

◆ Peel pineapple and remove central core. Pour vodka into a shallow dish, add pineapple slices, then turn slices over once. Cover dish and leave to marinate 20 minutes.

◆ Melt butter in a small pan. Remove from heat and stir in cream, cardamom and confectioners' sugar.

◆ Dip pineapple slices into melted butter mixture and grill over hot coals 5 minutes on each side until golden brown.

◆ Serve on warm plates, with pineapple centers filled with morello cherries. Dust lightly with confectioners' sugar.

Tamarillos with Brown Sugar

MAKES 4 SERVINGS

4 RIPE TAMARILLOS, HALVED

3 TABLESPOONS BROWN SUGAR

VANILLA ICE CREAM,
TO SERVE (OPTIONAL)

◆ Place 2 tamarillo halves on a piece of double-thickness aluminum foil. Sprinkle with one quarter of the brown sugar and fold foil over to produce a package. Repeat with remaining tamarillos and sugar to produce 4 individual packages.

◆ Cook tamarillo packages on the grill about 10 minutes, until they are warmed through and sugar has melted.

◆ Serve at once, with scoops of vanilla ice cream, if desired.

Almond-stuffed Medjool Dates

MAKES 2 TO 4 SERVINGS

12 LARGE FRESH MEDJOOL DATES

½ CUP (3 OUNCES) ALMONDS,
TOASTED

2 TABLESPOONS MASCARPONE CHEESE
OR CREAM CHEESE

¼ CUP BRANDY

1 CINNAMON STICK,
BROKEN IN HALF

2 TABLESPOONS SOFT BROWN SUGAR

¼ CUP FRESHLY SQUEEZED
ORANGE JUICE

PLAIN YOGURT,
TO SERVE

◆ Make a slit in the side of each date and remove and discard pits. Reserve 12 whole almonds and finely chop the remainder.

◆ Place chopped almonds in a bowl and add mascarpone cheese and 2 tablespoons brandy. Mix well to combine. Fill dates with mixture and add a whole almond to each cavity.

◆ Place 6 dates and half a cinnamon stick on a large piece of double-thickness aluminum foil.

◆ Mix remaining brandy, brown sugar and orange juice together. Spoon half the mixture over the dates.

◆ Wrap up foil to produce a package. Repeat with remaining dates, cinnamon and orange juice mixture.

◆ Cook foil packages on the grill about 10 minutes, until dates are tender and warmed through. Serve with yogurt.

Pear with Chocolate Sauce

◆ Cream together ricotta cheese, ground hazelnuts, honey, egg yolks and crushed cardamom seeds.

◆ Peel pears. Cut a thin slice from base of each pear and, using a corer or small spoon, carefully scoop out core as far up inside the pear as possible, without damaging the flesh.

◆ Fill cavities with ricotta mixture, pressing in well. Smooth bottoms flat. Place pears on individual pieces of double-thickness aluminum foil and twist at the tops to secure fillings.

◆ Grill over medium coals 20 to 30 minutes, until pears are cooked.

◆ Just before pears are ready, make sauce. Place chocolate, butter, brandy and thick sour cream in a small pan and heat gently until melted. Stir well and keep warm.

◆ Transfer pears to serving plates, slice in half to reveal filling, and pour over sauce. Serve immediately.

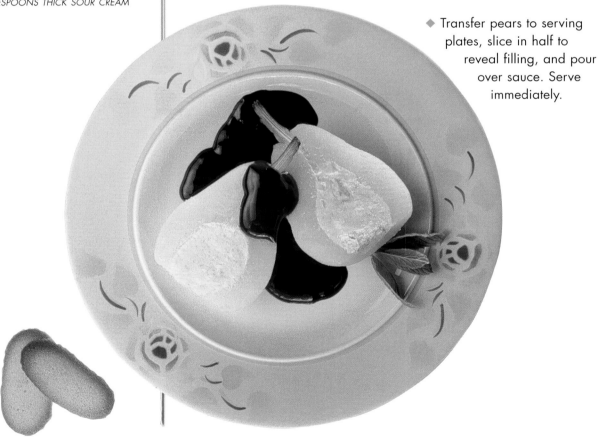

Dips and Sauces

Avocado and Chile Dip

1 FAT GREEN FRESH CHILE

2 MEDIUM-SIZE RIPE AVOCADOS

GRATED PEEL 1 LIME

1 TABLESPOON LIME JUICE

3 TABLESPOONS FINELY CHOPPED MIXED FRESH HERBS (E.G. LOVAGE, ARUGULA, SORREL, SAVORY, THYME, PARSLEY, BASIL, CHIVES, TARRAGON)

⅓ CUP (3 OUNCES) RICOTTA CHEESE

1 GARLIC CLOVE, CRUSHED

2 TEASPOONS GREEN PEPPERCORNS, CRUSHED

¼ TEASPOON COARSE SEA SALT

HERB SPRIGS, TO GARNISH

◆ Place chile on the grill over hot coals 5 to 8 minutes, turning frequently, until skin blisters and blackens. Remove skin and seeds and chop flesh roughly.

◆ Peel avocados and chop flesh roughly. Mix with lime juice to prevent discoloration.

◆ Place avocado in a blender or food processor with chile, lime peel, mixed fresh herbs, ricotta cheese, garlic, green peppercorns and sea salt and blend until smooth. Season to taste, adding more lime juice if necessary.

◆ Pour or spoon dip into a serving bowl and garnish with sprigs of herbs. If not serving immediately, sprinkle with lime juice, cover tightly with plastic wrap and chill in the refrigerator.

Chargrilled Tomato and Chile Sauce

MAKES 3½ CUPS

7 (2 POUNDS) PLUM TOMATOES

*4 LARGE GARLIC CLOVES,
UNPEELED*

2 FRESH GREEN CHILES

2 TEASPOONS DRIED OREGANO OR THYME

2 TABLESPOONS OLIVE OIL

½ ONION, FINELY CHOPPED

½ TEASPOON SUGAR

½ TEASPOON SALT

FRESHLY GROUND BLACK PEPPER

1 TABLESPOON (½ OUNCE) BUTTER

◆ Place tomatoes, garlic and chiles on the grill over hot coals. Turn frequently, until skins blister and blacken. (Chiles will need about 5 minutes, garlic 10 minutes and tomatoes 15 minutes.)

◆ Peel garlic, remove skin and seeds from chile, but do not peel tomatoes.

◆ Dry-fry oregano in a small heavy-bottomed pan a few minutes until you can smell the aroma.

◆ Heat oil in another small pan. Gently fry onion about 5 minutes until translucent. Add oregano and fry another minute.

◆ Purée tomatoes, including any blackened bits of skin (they add to the flavor), with garlic, chile and onion mixture until smooth.

◆ Pour into a large skillet and season with sugar, salt and freshly ground black pepper. Simmer 5 to 10 minutes, stirring occasionally, until some of the liquid has evaporated. Stir in butter.

Skordalia

MAKES 1 CUP

2 SLICES DAY-OLD WHITE BREAD,
CUBED

¼ CUP MILK

2 GARLIC CLOVES, CRUSHED

2 TEASPOONS SEA SALT

DASH CAYENNE PEPPER

⅓ CUP EXTRA VIRGIN OLIVE OIL

1 TABLESPOON LEMON JUICE

◆ Soak bread in milk 5 minutes. Squeeze out milk and place bread in a blender or food processor. Add garlic, sea salt and cayenne pepper and blend until smooth.

◆ Gradually blend in oil and 1 tablespoon boiling water to form a thick sauce. Stir in lemon juice and season to taste.

◆ Refrigerate and use within two days.

Olive and Cilantro Relish

MAKES 4 SERVINGS

2 RED BELL PEPPERS

1 CUP (6 OUNCES) PITTED AND FINELY
SLICED RIPE OLIVES

½ FRESH GREEN CHILE,
SEEDED AND VERY FINELY CHOPPED

6 TABLESPOONS FINELY CHOPPED
CILANTRO LEAVES

1 TABLESPOON LEMON JUICE

FRESHLY GROUND BLACK PEPPER

⅓ CUP OLIVE OIL

SALAD LEAVES, TO SERVE

1 HARD-BOILED EGG,
QUARTERED, TO SERVE

◆ Place peppers on the grill over hot coals 10 minutes, turning occasionally, until skins begin to blacken. Cover or place in a sealed plastic bag 5 minutes.

◆ Remove skin and seeds and cut flesh into small dice. Mix with olives, chile and cilantro in a bowl.

◆ Whisk together lemon juice, freshly ground black pepper and olive oil and pour over olive mixture. Allow to stand at room temperature 1 hour.

◆ Pile mixture on a bed of salad leaves and top with hard-cooked egg quarters to serve.

Garbanzo Bean and Eggplant Dip

MAKES 4 SERVINGS

2 SMALL EGGPLANTS

½ CUP (3 OUNCES) GARBANZO BEANS,
SOAKED OVERNIGHT

¼ TEASPOON SALT

6 TABLESPOONS PLAIN YOGURT

GRATED PEEL ½ LIME

2 TABLESPOONS LIME JUICE

1 GARLIC CLOVE, CRUSHED

2 TABLESPOONS OLIVE OIL

DASH CAYENNE PEPPER

RIPE OLIVES, TO GARNISH

DASH CAYENNE PEPPER,
TO GARNISH

◆ Cook eggplants on grill over hot coals 5 to 20 minutes, turning occasionally until charred. Allow to cool slightly, then remove skin. Squeeze out bitter juices then let drain.

◆ Place garbanzo beans in large pan of water. Bring to a boil and simmer about 20 minutes until soft. Add salt halfway through cooking time.

◆ Drain garbanzo beans and purée in a blender or food processor with eggplants, yogurt, lime peel and juice, garlic, olive oil and cayenne pepper.

◆ Transfer to a bowl and garnish with olives and cayenne pepper.

Roasted Red Bell Pepper Sauce

MAKES 3½ CUPS

3 RED BELL PEPPERS

3 ORANGE BELL PEPPERS

3 TABLESPOONS OLIVE OIL

4 SHALLOTS, CHOPPED

2 GARLIC CLOVES, CRUSHED

1¼ CUPS VEGETABLE STOCK

1 TABLESPOON RED WINE VINEGAR

1 TEASPOON CASTER SUGAR

SALT AND FRESHLY GROUND BLACK PEPPER

◆ Cook peppers over hot coals 10 minutes, turning occasionally, until skins begin to blacken.

◆ Cover or place in a sealed plastic bag 5 minutes. Peel away skin, remove seeds and chop flesh coarsely.

◆ Heat oil in a pan and cook and stir shallots and garlic 4 to 5 minutes until softened.

◆ Add peppers, stock, vinegar, sugar and seasoning, and cook mixture, uncovered, 10 to 15 minutes until liquid has reduced slightly.

◆ Allow mixture to cool and then purée in a blender or food processor to produce a smooth, thick sauce. Taste and adjust seasoning if necessary.

◆ The sauce will keep fresh 4 to 5 days stored in the refrigerator.

Spicy Tomato Sauce

MAKES 3½ CUPS

8 (2 POUNDS) RIPE TOMATOES

3 GARLIC CLOVES, UNPEELED

3 TABLESPOONS OLIVE OIL

3 TO 4 FRESH RED CHILES, SEEDED AND FINELY CHOPPED

2 SHALLOTS, FINELY CHOPPED

1 TEASPOON SUPERFINE SUGAR

SALT AND FRESHLY GROUND BLACK PEPPER

◆ Cook tomatoes and garlic cloves on the grill over medium coals, turning occasionally, about 10 minutes. The tomatoes are ready when they have softened and their skins begin to char. The garlic should be browned and soft.

◆ Remove tomatoes and garlic cloves from the grill and allow to cool. Peel garlic and mash flesh. Do not peel tomatoes, but chop roughly.

◆ Heat oil in a pan and add chiles and shallots. Cook 5 minutes. Add tomatoes, garlic, sugar and salt and pepper to the pan and stir, uncovered, 15 minutes, until the sauce is thick.

◆ Allow sauce to cool, then purée in a blender or food processor until smooth. Taste and adjust seasoning as necessary.

◆ The sauce will keep fresh 4 to 5 days stored in the refrigerator. It makes the perfect pizza topping or a sauce for calzone.

Grilled Corn Salsa

2 LARGE EARS CORN

1 RED OR LARGE SWEET ONION, FINELY CHOPPED

4 RIPE PLUM TOMATOES, SEEDED AND COARSELY CHOPPED

1 GARLIC CLOVE, FINELY CHOPPED

2 JALAPIÑO CHILES, SEEDED AND FINELY CHOPPED

1 BUNCH CILANTRO, TRIMMED AND FINELY CHOPPED

SALT AND FRESHLY GROUND BLACK PEPPER

◆ Cook corn in boiling water about 15 minutes, until tender. Drain.

◆ Place corn on grill over hot coals and cook, turning occasionally, about 10 minutes. Let cool.

◆ Hold 1 ear of corn vertically at a slight angle to a chopping board, stem end down. Using a sharp knife, cut down along ear to remove kernels. Place kernels in a large bowl and repeat with remaining corn.

◆ Using a sharp knife, scrape along each ear, removing remaining 'milk' and add this to the bowl. Stir in onion.

◆ Add tomatoes, garlic, chiles, cilantro, salt and black pepper. Toss together and spoon into a serving bowl.

◆ Let stand about 30 minutes before serving.

Baba Ganoush

MAKES 6 SERVINGS

2 SMALL EGGPLANTS

1 GARLIC CLOVE, CRUSHED

¼ CUP TAHINI

½ CUP (1 OUNCE) GROUND ALMONDS

JUICE ½ LEMON

½ TEASPOON GROUND CUMIN

SALT AND FRESHLY GROUND BLACK PEPPER

1 TABLESPOON CHOPPED FRESH MINT

2 TABLESPOONS OLIVE OIL

FRESH MINT LEAVES, TO GARNISH

SELECTION OF VEGETABLES, SUCH AS BABY ARTICHOKES, RADISHES, SLICED BELL PEPPERS, TO SERVE

◆ Cook eggplants on a rack over hot coals, turning often, until black and blistered.

◆ Remove skins, chop flesh roughly and let drain in a colander 10 minutes.

◆ Squeeze out as much liquid from eggplants as possible and place flesh in a food processor or blender.

◆ Add garlic, tahini, ground almonds, lemon juice, cumin, salt and freshly ground black pepper and process to a smooth paste. Stir chopped mint leaves into dip.

◆ Spoon into a serving bowl and drizzle with olive oil. Scatter mint leaves on top. Place bowl on a serving platter and serve with a selection of vegetables.

Index